CHEERFUL by DESIGN

A Guide to Authentic Happiness & Well-Being

FATIMA RUIZ

Copyright © 2021 by Fatima Ruiz

All Rights Reserved. No part of this publication may be reproduced or transmitted in any form or by any means without written permission of the publisher.

ISBN: 978-0-9909428-1-8

Book Cover and interior design by Najdan Mancic

For my husband Israel and children, Aneela, Isaac & Ivan.

"

SPREAD LOVE EVERYWHERE YOU GO.
LET NO ONE EVER COME TO YOU
WITHOUT LEAVING HAPPIER.

—MOTHER TERESA

THIS WORKBOOK BELONGS TO:

....

"

THIS IS THE BEGINNING OF THE HAPPINESS
AND WELL-BEING YOU TRULY DESERVE

—FATIMA RUIZ

TABLE OF CONTENTS

MINI LESSON 1: *What Is Positive Psychology?* 9
   HAPPINESS ACTIVITY 1: *The Good Things in Life* 11

MINI LESSON 2: *Gratitude* 13
   HAPPINESS ACTIVITY 2: *Gratitude Letter* 15
   HAPPINESS ACTIVITY 3: *Gratitude Journal* 16

MINI LESSON 3: *Kindness* 18
   HAPPINESS ACTIVITY 4: *Random Acts of Kindness* 20

MINI LESSON 4: *Social Connections* 22
   HAPPINESS ACTIVITY 5: *Active Listening* 24

MINI LESSON 5: *Mindfulness & Meditation* 26
   HAPPINESS ACTIVITY 6: *Let's Meditate* 29
   HAPPINESS ACTIVITY 7: *The Orange* 32
   HAPPINESS ACTIVITY 8: *Nature Walk* 34

MINI LESSON 6: *Forgiveness* 35
   HAPPINESS ACTIVITY 10: *Forgiveness Letter* 37

MINI LESSON 7: *Achieving FLOW for Happiness* 38
   FLOW CHECKER 40

MINI LESSON 8: *Self-Compassion* 41
   HAPPINESS ACTIVITY 12: *Letter to Self* 43

MINI LESSON 9: *Physical Activity & Happiness* 44
   HAPPINESS ACTIVITY 13: *Create a Fitness Routine* 47

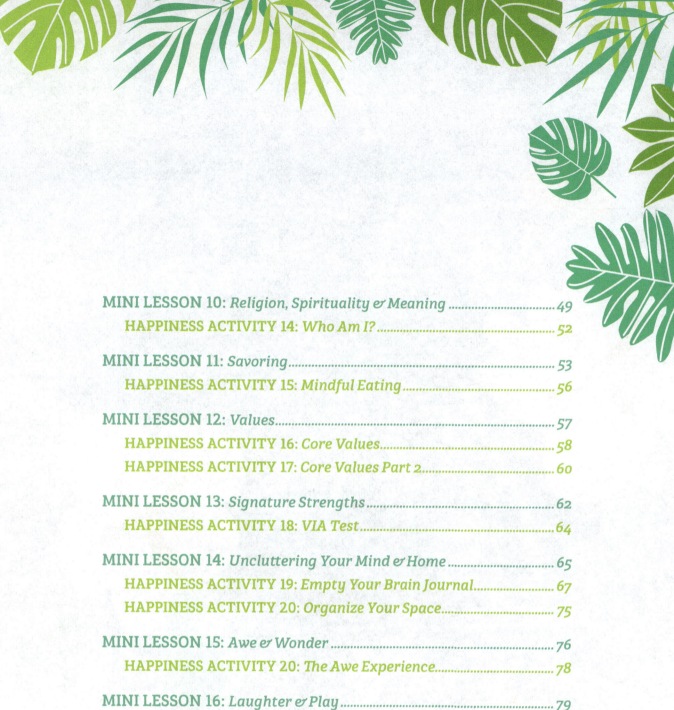

MINI LESSON 10: *Religion, Spirituality & Meaning* 49
   HAPPINESS ACTIVITY 14: *Who Am I?* 52

MINI LESSON 11: *Savoring* 53
   HAPPINESS ACTIVITY 15: *Mindful Eating* 56

MINI LESSON 12: *Values* 57
   HAPPINESS ACTIVITY 16: *Core Values* 58
   HAPPINESS ACTIVITY 17: *Core Values Part 2* 60

MINI LESSON 13: *Signature Strengths* 62
   HAPPINESS ACTIVITY 18: *VIA Test* 64

MINI LESSON 14: *Uncluttering Your Mind & Home* 65
   HAPPINESS ACTIVITY 19: *Empty Your Brain Journal* 67
   HAPPINESS ACTIVITY 20: *Organize Your Space* 75

MINI LESSON 15: *Awe & Wonder* 76
   HAPPINESS ACTIVITY 20: *The Awe Experience* 78

MINI LESSON 16: *Laughter & Play* 79
   HAPPINESS ACTIVITY 22: *It's time to Laugh & Play* 81

MINI LESSON 17: *Goals* 82
   HAPPINESS ACTIVITY 23: *My Future Self* 85
   HAPPINESS ACTIVITY 24: *Goal Setting* 86

52-WEEK WORKBOOK 89

REFERENCES 143

MINI LESSON 1
WHAT IS POSITIVE PSYCHOLOGY?

POSITIVE PSYCHOLOGY IS a branch of psychology that studies exactly what helps people to flourish and live happy, fulfilling lives (Gable & Haidt, 2005). While historically, psychological study has placed a strong emphasis on mental illness and maladaptive behavior, practitioners of positive psychology seek instead to emphasize and build upon people's strengths, positive character traits, and positive emotional states.

One psychologist (and well-known proponent of positive psychology), Dr. Christopher Peterson, defined positive psychology as "the scientific study of what goes right in life" (Peterson, 2009, p.3).

Proponents of positive psychology understand that good mental health is about more than an absence of mental illness. To truly achieve good mental health, one must have the ability to thrive, even in the face of adversity. Of course, life comes with unavoidable challenges, but practitioners of positive psychology believe that we need to switch our focus to the things that make life worth living, despite those challenges.

Benefits of Positive Psychology

Positive psychology is an applied science. This means that this branch of psychology uses scientific research to achieve practical results. Practitioners of positive psychology are not only concerned with understanding the mechanisms behind happiness and other positive emotional states; they want to use the information they've gained through scientific research to actually improve people's lives.

Randomized control trials have been conducted to study the effectiveness of positive psychology and the activities that it promotes (Seligman & Steen, et. al, 2005). The evidence from these studies has shown us that positive psychology actually has proven health benefits. According to the research, using positive psychology activities (like practicing gratitude or entering flow) to promote a sense of purpose, feelings of happiness, and optimism leads to:

- Increased happiness
- Less depression symptoms
- Stronger immune system
- Better heart health, including lower blood pressure
- Longer life
- More fulfilling relationships
- Better lung function
- Better cancer outcomes (Park & Peterson, 2016)

As we move into the future of positive psychology, research is sure to reveal to us further health benefits of living a life filled with kindness, gratitude & Flow.

HAPPINESS ACTIVITY 1

THE GOOD THINGS IN LIFE

For one week, write down three things that went well for you each day, and write down why they went well.

MONDAY

What: ....
Why: ....

What: ....
Why: ....

What: ....
Why: ....

TUESDAY

What: ....
Why: ....

What: ....
Why: ....

What: ....
Why: ....

WEDNESDAY

What: ....
Why: ....

What: ....
Why: ....

What: ....
Why: ....

THURSDAY

What: ....
Why: ....

What: ....
Why: ....

What: ....
Why: ....

FRIDAY

What: ....
Why: ....

What: ....
Why: ....

What: ....
Why: ....

SATURDAY

What: ....
Why: ....

What: ....
Why: ....

What: ....
Why: ....

SUNDAY

What: ....
Why: ....

What: ....
Why: ....

What: ....
Why: ....

MINI LESSON 2
GRATITUDE

The Benefits of Gratitude

NOT ONLY DOES practicing gratitude feel good in the moment, but it's also been scientifically tied to tangible benefits for both our physical and mental health. Dr. Robert Emmons, who we can thank for most of the groundbreaking research that's been conducted on the benefits of gratitude, has consistently found that gratitude increases overall well-being, improves health, and leads to more prosocial behavior (Emmons & Mishra, 2013).

Some of the life-changing benefits of gratitude include:

- A stronger immune system
- Improved mental health (including fewer symptoms of depression and anxiety)
- Better relationships
- A more optimistic life outlook
- More empathy for others
- Better sleep
- Higher self-esteem
- Less chronic pain
- More mental strength and emotional resiliency (Harvard Health Publishing, 2011).

Mindfulness & Gratitude

Mindfulness is an ancient Buddhist practice. More recently it's been applied to Western psychological practice. At its essence, it's simply the practice of being completely present in the now. This is how Emmons suggests we incorporate more gratitude into our lives—just by noticing opportunities to do so (Bono et. al, 2012).

To apply mindfulness to the practice of gratitude, get into the habit of being fully present in each moment. Sometimes, when we can't find anything to be grateful for, it's simply because we're not paying enough attention. When you start being mindful, you'll start noticing the little things, like the beautiful butterfly in your garden or the smell of freshly baked bread.

There's So Much to Be Grateful For

If we look closely enough, our lives are full of things to be grateful for. Science has shown us that learning to intentionally foster gratitude helps us become healthier, happier people.

HAPPINESS ACTIVITY 2
GRATITUDE LETTER

Write a letter to a friend, family member or coworker thanking them for something they have done to impact your life in a positive way. Call them and read the letter or send it to them. The important thing is that they know how much you appreciate them.

DEAR: ....

THANK YOU FOR:
....
....
....
....
....
....
....
....
....
....

HAPPINESS ACTIVITY 3
GRATITUDE JOURNAL

MONDAY
1. ......
2. ......
3. ......
4. ......
5. ......

TUESDAY
1. ......
2. ......
3. ......
4. ......
5. ......

WEDNESDAY
1. ......
2. ......
3. ......
4. ......
5. ......

THURSDAY

1. ....
2. ....
3. ....
4. ....
5. ....

FRIDAY

1. ....
2. ....
3. ....
4. ....
5. ....

SATURDAY

1. ....
2. ....
3. ....
4. ....
5. ....

SUNDAY

1. ....
2. ....
3. ....
4. ....
5. ....

MINI LESSON 3
KINDNESS

Does Being Kind Make You Happier?

WE'VE ALL SEEN the feel-good news stories: someone pays for a stranger's cup of coffee, and another gives a $100 tip to their food server. Random acts of kindness are all over social media, and it's obvious these kinds of actions make a big difference to the people on the receiving end.

But what about the person performing the act of kindness? Does being kind to strangers make us happier people?

Research tells us that yes—acts of kindness not only benefit the receiver, but the giver as well.

The Benefits of Kindness

Dr. Sonja Lyobomirsky, a well-known researcher in the field of positive psychology, studies how different actions can improve our happiness and well-being.

In one study, she asked her participants to commit to performing five acts of kindness every week for six weeks. It didn't matter what the act of kindness was; it could be as small as holding the door open for a pregnant stranger or as large as giving money away.

The study found that people who completed all five acts of kindness in one day (rather than one per day for five days) experienced an increase in happiness (Lyubomirsky, Shelson, & Schkade, 2005). Having some variety in the acts they performed also made a difference.

These results suggest that performing random acts of kindness *can* make a difference in our lives—but if we're just completing the *same* act every once in a while, then we might not be able to really savor how good it feels. In fact, if we're forced to do the same act of kindness over and over again, we can start to see it as a chore—and it can even make us *less* happy (Sheldon, Boehm, & Lyubomirsky, 2013).

It might be a good idea to set aside some time on the same day every week to perform your acts of kindness. And make sure you're not doing the same act of kindness over and over again—because that could become unsatisfying.

After you perform your act of kindness, write a few sentences on what you did, and how it made you feel. This will help you to savor the moment and enjoy the feelings of happiness that the random act of kindness brings.

Being Kind Helps Others—and You

The Dalai Lama famously said, "If you want others to be happy, practice compassion. If you want to be happy, practice compassion." It turns out he was right—by performing random acts of kindness, we can make a difference in the world *and* become happier people.

HAPPINESS ACTIVITY 4
RANDOM ACTS OF KINDNESS

The acts of kindness you choose to perform can be big or small. Here are some ideas to get you started:

- Compliment someone.
- Pay for someone's coffee.
- Let another car in your lane in traffic.
- Give someone your seat on the bus.
- Fill up someone's expired parking meter.
- Volunteer at a soup kitchen.
- Give money to a person without a home.
- Let someone who's in a hurry cut in front of you at the grocery store.
- Cook a meal for a neighbor.
- Offer to babysit your friend's children.
- Publicly offer recognition to a coworker.

ACTS OF KINDNESS THIS WEEK

1. ....
....

2. ....
....

3. ....
....

4. ....
....

5. ....
....

How did you feel after completing the acts of kindness?

....

....

....

....

MINI LESSON 4
SOCIAL CONNECTIONS

Could Social Connection Be the Key to Happiness?

WE ALL LOVE and value our family and friends. We appreciate them and enjoy spending time with them. But research shows that we should be appreciating them even more, and that having strong social connections is one of the primary predicting factors for happiness (Eid & Larson, 2008).

What does the evidence say?

More and more, scientific research is pointing toward the idea that having strong personal relationships in our lives is absolutely key to increasing happiness. Study after study, all around the world, has proven this—people who engage in more fulfilling social activities are, overall, happier than their more individualistic or solitary counterparts.

Research that's been conducted on happiness and life satisfaction for older adults has revealed similar results. Studies show that older adults who have strong social relationships are not only happier, but also live longer, healthier lives (Rook & Charles, 2017).

Social support is so key in finding happiness that it's even been shown to mitigate the effects of some negative life events, including unemployment (Helliwell, et. al, 2020).

Across the world, the findings are similar. One annual study called the *World Happiness Report* measures each country's level of social support by looking at its citizens' answers to the Gallup poll question; "If you were in trouble, do you have relatives or friends you could count on to help whenever you needed them, or not?"

The report found that social support had a greater effect on the results of the Cantril ladder (a tool that measures well-being, life satisfaction, and happiness) than any other variable, including the country's GDP, freedom to make life choices, and perceptions of corruption. Nordic countries like Finland and Denmark consistently rank as some of the happiest countries in the world, and there are a few things they have in common—including high levels of social support (Helliwell, et. al, 2020).

Social connection makes us happier. Period.

The Harvard Study of Adult Development is an ongoing research project that has studied the lives of two groups of men for over 75 years. The researchers interview their subjects to understand more deeply what factors truly lead to happy and healthy lives (Vaillant, 2012).

Robert Waldinger, the current director of the study, says that above all, what they've learned is this: "Good relationships keep us happier and healthier. Period." (Waldinger, 2015).

The next time you become stressed about not being rich enough or accomplished enough, try to remember this very important lesson. At the end of the day, it's less about what we do in life, and more about who we do it with.

HAPPINESS ACTIVITY 5
ACTIVE LISTENING

Listening is one of the most important skills you can have. How well you listen has a major effect on the quality of your relationships with others. One practice that's been shown to increase happiness is active listening. Take 15-30 minutes this week to have a conversation with someone you're close to and ask them to share what's on their mind. Here are a few tips to ensure you are a great listener.

- Give your undivided attention (don't think about how you are going to respond or how the conversation relates to you).
- Use your body to show you are listening (nod, smile, lean-in and acknowledge what your speaker is saying with an occasional *yes* or *uh huh*.
- Don't immediately judge what they are saying.
- Don't interrupt them; wait and ask reflective questions like, "What I'm hearing is... ,"

Reflect On Your Experience:

MINI LESSON 5
MINDFULNESS & MEDITATION

What Are the Benefits of Meditation?

MORE AND MORE people are tuning into the benefits of a daily meditation practice. Supporters of this ancient spiritual tradition say that it helps them feel more relaxed, less stressed, and happier overall.

What Is Meditation?

Although its image is changing in modern times, it used to be that the word "meditation" would bring to mind the image of a Buddhist monk, hiding away in a cave somewhere and sitting perfectly still. Although the practice of meditation does have its roots in Eastern spiritual practices like Buddhism, anyone can practice it. It is not always a religious practice, and you can meditate no matter what faith you identify with.

Meditation, at its essence, is the practice of calming the mind to gain insight into reality or simply to relax. There are many different types of meditation, including:

- MANTRA MEDITATION: This type of meditation is often used as part of a bigger spiritual practice. The meditator chooses a syllable, word, or phrase as the object of meditation.

- LOVING KINDNESS MEDITATION: This meditation uses words and images that promote love and kindness toward yourself and others. Practitioners of loving kindness meditation are better able to forgive, connect to others and love themselves more deeply.
- SILENT MEDITATION: In this meditation technique, you remain silent for the duration of the meditation, clearing you mind and bringing peace and inner joy to your life.

What is Mindfulness?

According to Mindful.org, "mindfulness is the basic human ability to be fully present, aware of where we are and what we're doing, and not overly reactive or overwhelmed by what's going on around us."

- MINDFULNESS MEDITATION: This is the most studied form of meditation in psychological research. Mindfulness meditation involves learning to be completely present in the here and now. Often, people pay close attention to their breath during mindfulness meditation.

Health Benefits of Meditation

Studies show that meditating in general has numerous health benefits, including:

- Less pain. A study conducted in 2016 found that regular meditators were able to control their pain better than non-meditators (Reiner, Tibi, & Lipsitz, 2013).

- Lower blood pressure and better heart health. There's evidence that supports the idea that meditation lowers our overall stress levels, which in turn leads to lower blood pressure and a stronger heart (Goldstein et. al, 2012).

- Improved gastrointestinal symptoms. Some studies have found that meditating lessens the symptoms of certain gastrointestinal diseases, including ulcerative colitis and irritable bowel syndrome (Gaylord et. al, 2011).

- Better mental health: Meditation is most often used to improve mental health. Meditation, especially mindfulness meditation, has been found to decrease symptoms of depression, anxiety, and insomnia (Goyal et. al, 2014).

Mindfulness meditation has numerous health benefits for both clinical and non-clinical populations. By starting a regular meditation practice, you could become a healthier, happier, and more relaxed person.

HAPPINESS ACTIVITY 6
LET'S MEDITATE

This week, you will practice the three types of meditation mentioned in this mini lesson (See meditations on following page). After you've tried each type of meditation, pick your favorite, and continue meditating for the duration of the week. You can find good meditation videos on YouTube. I have also provided you some basic instructions.

Basic meditation instructions to prepare you for all three meditation types:

1. Find a quiet place in your home, car or outside. The key is not to be interrupted.
2. Sit in a comfortable position on the floor or on a chair. You can also laydown, just make sure you are comfortable.
3. Keep your back straight, arms resting on your lap.
4. Close your eyes and take a deep breath in through you nose and out through your mouth.
5. Focus on the point between your eyebrows, your breath or prefrontal lobe.
6. Now, take a breath in through your nose for 6 seconds, hold it for about 6 seconds and release it for 6 seconds. (The actual number of seconds depend on your comfort level.)
7. Repeat this breathing technique for 3 or more breathing cycles.
8. Finally, take one more deep breath in through your nose and out through your mouth, exhaling the words *Ha, Ha, Haaaaa*.
9. Keep your eyes closed and focus on your breath.

Mantra Meditation

As you sit, repeat a mantra or affirmation silently in your head. Some examples of mantras include; Hong-Sau (*I am Spirit*), *I am peace*, *I am love* or any other mantra or affirmation that speaks to your heart.

Silent Meditation

During a silent meditation, you sit quietly, silently observing your breath. Sometimes it helps to focus on the humming of an air conditioning unit or other gentle neutral noise that doesn't bring up any thoughts or concerns.

Loving-Kindness Meditation

For this type of meditation, you first focus on yourself, repeating the words: *I am healthy, I am happy, I am peaceful, I am loved*. Next you focus on someone in your life that you love and want to send loving thoughts towards, repeating the words: You are healthy, you are happy, you are peaceful and you are loved. Now, think of someone in your life (picture them) that you are having difficulty with and repeat the mantra above. Finally, think of a person (picture them) in your life that could really use some peace and love right now and repeat the mantra above.

MONDAY
....
....

TUESDAY
....
....

WEDNESDAY
....
....

THURSDAY
....
....

FRIDAY
....
....

SATURDAY
....
....

SUNDAY
....
....

Write down the type of meditation used on each day this week

HAPPINESS ACTIVITY 7
THE ORANGE

The Raisin Exercise was developed by Jon Kabat-Zinn, PhD, the creator of mindfulness-based stress reduction. This exercise keeps you in the present moment. It also teaches you to savor your food and participate in mindful eating.

- Take an orange in your hand. Observe its shape, color, and pores.
- Bring it closer to your face and spend a few more moments examining its shape, and texture.
- Now, apply slight pressure to your orange. How does it feel? Is it firm, soft, or somewhere in the middle? It is cold or warm to the touch?
- Smell the orange. What is its aroma? Can you smell the citrus?
- Next, bring the orange to your ear. Does it make any noise if you rub it or squeeze it?
- Finally, peel your orange and take another whiff. Did the aroma of the orange change? Now, put the orange in your mouth and savor it. What sensations does it create? Notice as it travels down your throat and into your stomach.

Write about your experience:

HAPPINESS ACTIVITY 8
NATURE WALK

Find a peaceful place to take a short walk in nature.

Nature Walk

As you walk, allow your senses to take in everything around you. What do you see—trees, flowers, grass, or maybe tiny insects moving about? Is there anything you can feel? Maybe a slight breeze, the coolness of a shaded path or the warmth of the sun? Can you hear anything? Are there any distinctive smells? Notice everything around you.

Write about your experience:

....
....
....
....
....
....
....
....

MINI LESSON 6
FORGIVENESS

WHEN SOMEONE HAS wronged us, it's tempting to hold on to that grudge forever. We don't do it out of spite; rather, we feel so angry and betrayed that we feel like we simply can't get past it. We might have thoughts like, "Why should I forgive him? He's the one that did something wrong," or, "I won't let them take advantage of me like that. If I forgive them, the bad thing might happen to me again."

Of course, it's understandable not to want to get hurt again, and it's possible that refusing to forgive the person who hurt us makes us feel more protected in some way. But scientific research actually shows us that to forgive isn't something that we should do for the benefit of the person who hurt us—forgiving others makes us healthier, happier people.

What Forgiveness is—and What it Isn't

Many of us hold the erroneous idea that you forgiving someone means allowing them the freedom to not take responsibility for their actions. We might feel like forgiving someone who hurt us means they are "getting away with it" in some way.

Many people think this way, but this is not what forgiveness is all about. The exact definition of forgiveness often slightly differs across studies, but most positive psychologists agree that forgiveness is, in essence, a deliberate decision to let go of any anger or lingering resentment that you feel internally towards someone. Forgiveness could be towards another person, a group of people, or even towards yourself.

What forgiveness is not is forgetting the terrible thing that happened to you, excusing or condoning someone's hurtful actions, or allowing them to "get away with" the hurtful act without taking any responsibility for it.

How Does Forgiveness Help You?

In research studies, the act of forgiveness has been linked to better health and well-being. It isn't hard to imagine why: Think about how you feel when you recall an old enemy or a grudge. Most people feel angry when they think in this way, and anger has been linked to high stress and all its consequences.

On the other hand, when we can let go of this resentment and forgive the person, we reap the health rewards. These include better heart health, lower blood pressure, a stronger immune system, and other benefits of less stress (Toussaint, et. al, 2016). Forgiveness has even been linked to less lower back pain (Carson et. al, 2005). On top of this, people who are able to forgive tend to feel less negative emotions than people who can't forgive (Marks et. al, 2013).

Forgiveness is especially important when it comes to romantic relationships. Couples who know how to forgive each other quickly are reported to be happier in their marriages, even many weeks after the forgiveness happens (Braithwaite, Selby, & Fincham, 2011). When you intentionally refrain from harboring feelings of anger or resentment about someone, then you free yourself from this emotional baggage.

HAPPINESS ACTIVITY 10
FORGIVENESS LETTER

Write a forgiveness letter to someone who has hurt you. Include what happened to you that made you hurt. Think about your offender's circumstances, and why you think they did what they did. Lastly, reframe the experience and find some meaning or purpose in what occurred. Write this letter to someone who offended you at work or school. Continuing writing letters to others who have hurt you. When you're ready, end with the most egregious offences.

TO: ....

I FORGIVE YOU FOR:

....
....
....
....
....
....
....
....
....

MINI LESSON 7

ACHIEVING FLOW FOR HAPPINESS

What Is Flow, and How Can We Achieve It?

HAVE YOU EVER felt like you were completely "in the zone"? Maybe you were out for a jog, listening to a beautiful piece of music, or really productive on a project at work. Whatever you were doing, you probably felt completely present in the moment; maybe you were even able to forget about the stresses of daily life for a while.

This particular state-of-mind is something that psychologist and happiness researcher Mihaly Csikszentmihalyi has studied for decades. He calls it the "flow state," and he teaches that anyone is able to achieve it.

What Are the Characteristics of a Flow State?

When Csikszentmihalyi began to study creativity and happiness decades ago, he found that most artists, musicians, athletes, and other master craftsmen described entering into a similar mindset when they engaged in their work. Catholic monks, Navajo shepherds, and Italian farmers all talked about the same feeling of being "in the zone." Some of them described it as temporarily not existing, or being on automatic pilot; they didn't need to think so much about what they were doing.

They all described a feeling of serenity, confidence, and ecstasy (Csikszentmihalyi, 1975).

Csikszentmihalyi and his colleague Jeanne Nakamura named this state of mind "flow," and they sought to define it so that it could be measured in studies about happiness and life satisfaction (Csikszentmihalyi, 1990). When you're in a flow state, you feel ecstatic, exhilarated, and confident. Tasks that help you get into the flow state bring more meaning to your life.

According to Csikszentmihalyi, a flow state is defined by the following characteristics:

1. Being completely focused on the present moment.
2. Action and awareness merges: We are moving almost automatically, and no longer worry or stress about things in our lives.
3. The task at hand has clear goals and immediate feedback.
4. Feeling a sense of control over our actions
5. Experiencing a sense of timelessness
6. Letting go of awareness or sense of self (although after the task is finished, our sense of self is stronger)
7. Feeling that whatever we are doing is worthy or rewarding (Bonaiuto et. al, 2016).

"Once those conditions are present, what you are doing becomes worth doing for its own sake," Csikszentmihalyi says (Csikszentmihaly, 2004).

The more time we spend in a state of flow, the happier, more peaceful, and more successful we will be in our lives.

FLOW CHECKER

This week, write down any activities that made you feel completely present "in the zone," where you felt ecstatic, exhilarated, and confident.

- ....
- ....
- ....
- ....
- ....
- ....
- ....
- ....
- ....
- ....
- ....
- ....
- ....
- ....
- ....
- ....
- ....

MINI LESSON 8
SELF-COMPASSION

Can Self-Compassion Make You Happier?

WE OFTEN HEAR about the psychological benefits of generosity and compassion toward others. As the Dalai Lama once said: "If you want others to be happy, practice compassion. If you want to make yourself happy, practice compassion."

Although we often think about compassion as something we practice for other people, it's important that we don't neglect to be compassionate toward ourselves, too. Positive psychologists like Dr. Kristin Neff have studied the benefits of self-compassion and have found that it's a crucial part of our overall happiness and health.

So what is self-compassion, exactly, and how can we practice it to achieve these benefits?

What Is Self-Compassion?

Dr. Neff, in an interview with The Greater Good Science Center, described self-compassion as "treating yourself with the same type of kind, caring support and understanding that you would show to anyone you cared about." She continued, "most of us make incredibly harsh, cruel self-judgments that we would never make about a total stranger, let alone someone we cared about" (Marsh, 2012).

Dr. Neff has identified three core components of self-compassion. They are:

1. Self-kindness (vs. self-judgment; this is the practice of actively being kind and reassuring toward oneself)
2. Common humanity (vs. isolation; this is about remembering that you aren't the only person who is suffering, and that no one is perfect)
3. Mindfulness (vs. over-identification; this is the practice of observing, not denying or ignoring, your painful thoughts and feelings without becoming attached to them).

Self-compassion differs from self-esteem in the idea that it's not about inflating our own egos or focusing on our own uniqueness. Self-esteem is often about making a value judgment about ourselves: "I am good." Self-compassion is about seeing and caring for ourselves in a gentle way (Neff, 2011).

It's about realizing that we experience suffering, just like anyone else in the world—and treating ourselves with the same compassion that we would treat someone else with who was also suffering.

So many of us get lost in negative self-talk and critical thinking. But if we can be as generous, kind, and loving toward ourselves as we are with others, then we can become happier and more confident people.

HAPPINESS ACTIVITY 12
LETTER TO SELF

Identify something about yourself that makes you feel ashamed, insecure, or not good enough. Describe how it makes you feel. Write a letter to yourself expressing deep compassion for the part of you that brings up negative emotions. Make sure to love yourself unconditionally. Consider your life circumstances that could have contributed to this negative aspect of yourself. Ask yourself—Is there something you can do to improve this negative part of yourself? Is there a positive way to cope with it as you work to feel better? Write the answers to these questions down and return to them when you're in a better place. Keep practicing self-compassion.

DEAR: ....

....

....

....

....

....

....

....

....

MINI LESSON 9
PHYSICAL ACTIVITY & HAPPINESS

Why Physical Activity Is One of the Best Ways to Achieve Happiness

PHYSICAL EXERCISE HAS long been touted by medical practitioners as something that's necessary for a healthy lifestyle. We've all learned, time and time again, that exercise is important for both our cardiovascular and respiratory health, and that we should strive to move our bodies every day. We've even learned that physical exercise has mood-boosting benefits, and that moving is good for our mental health. But could physical exercise really, truly make us happier people? Positive psychologists—the world's happiness experts—say yes.

A Positive Psychologist's Take on Exercise

Couch potatoes around the world can let out a collective groan: even positive psychology researchers confirm that physical exercise is an extremely important part of building a happy life.

Positive psychologist Sonja Lyuobomirsky, the author of *The How of Happiness*, states: "Exercise may very well be the most effective instant happiness booster of all activities" (Lyubomirsky, 2007).

Indeed, physical exercise is not only an important part of achieving happiness but may be *the most* important thing. And exercising regularly is one of the habits that the happiest people engage in.

There are many reasons for this, and most of them have to do with how physical activity changes the brain. Exercising releases important brain chemicals, including dopamine and endocannabinoids, which interact with the pleasure and reward circuits of the brain (Robertson et. al, 2010). This makes us feel less stressed and more receptive to experiences that bring us joy.

Happiness Benefits of Physical Activity

Positive psychologists have been studying how regular physical activity can help us find more happiness in our lives. They've found that physical activity has numerous benefits for our happiness, including:

- Less stress
- Improved mood
- More optimism
- More feelings of joy
- Reduced symptoms of depression
- Synchronized movements in a group—a group dance or yoga class, for example—help us feel joy and bond with others in a powerful way
- Better relationships with friends and family
- Bringing couples closer together

- Reduced anxiety
- More courage and resiliency (McGonical, 2019).

Psychologist Dr. Kelly McGonigal writes in her book, *The Joy of Movement*: "Physical activity stands out in its ability to fulfill so many human needs, and that makes it worth considering as a fundamentally valuable endeavor. It is as if what is good in us is most easily activated or accessed through movement."

It's hard to build an exercise habit, but it may be worth it knowing that exercising is one of the most critical parts of living a happy, healthy, and connected life.

HAPPINESS ACTIVITY 13
CREATE A FITNESS ROUTINE

It's sometimes difficult to incorporate exercise into your life if you don't build it into your daily habits. It doesn't matter what physical activity you choose—the important thing is to get moving. Whether you choose to swim, dance, or jog, you can reap the health and happiness benefits of moving your body. And the benefits are available to you no matter how old you are or where you are in your physical exercise journey (Windle et. al, 2010). Using the list below, track which days and times work best for you. Strive to exercise at least 3-5 days per week for maximum happiness results.

Create a Fitness Routine

MONDAY
- Time of Day: ....
- Physical Activity: ....
- Duration: ....

TUESDAY
- Time of Day: ....
- Physical Activity: ....
- Duration: ....

WEDNESDAY

Time of Day: ....

Physical Activity: ....

Duration: ....

THURSDAY

Time of Day: ....

Physical Activity: ....

Duration: ....

FRIDAY

Time of Day: ....

Physical Activity: ....

Duration: ....

SATURDAY

Time of Day: ....

Physical Activity: ....

Duration: ....

SUNDAY

Time of Day: ....

Physical Activity: ....

Duration: ....

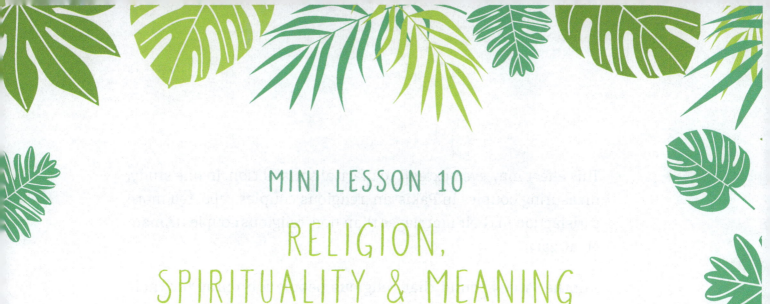

MINI LESSON 10

RELIGION, SPIRITUALITY & MEANING

The Psychological Benefits of Religion and Spirituality

IF YOU'RE A religious person, you may have directly experienced the happiness that your spiritual practice brings you. Maybe you feel at peace when you pray, or joyful when you attend church with people you love.

Recent research in the field of positive psychology has shown us that religious people might be onto something. The evidence tells us that practicing religion can have enormous benefits for mental health and relationships.

Here are 3 specific benefits that a spiritual practice can have for your well-being.

Better relationships

Studies have found that religion and spirituality improve people's social relationships. Belonging to a religious group is often the primary source of community for people, which leads to better social connection. Social connection is often studied in the field of positive psychology as a vital part of a happy life.

This effect may even extend to marital satisfaction. In one study, measuring couples in Pakistan, religious couples reported more satisfaction in their marriages than non-religious couples (Aman, et. al, 2019).

Another study found that religious people who pray for their partners feel more committed to the relationship (Fincham & Beach, 2014). And couples who report deeper spiritual intimacy and talk about their spiritual beliefs as a couple seem to deal with conflicts better (Kusner et. al, 2014).

Less depression

Religion and spirituality may also lead to decreased depression. One review found that well over half of the studies that have been conducted on the relationship between depression and religion reported that religious practice and depression have a negative correlation (Koenig, 2012).

This could be due to a number of different factors. People who practice religion also report higher rates of hope, optimism, meaning, and a sense of purpose. All of these feelings are likely to create more happiness and lead to less depression.

Perhaps because religious people face less depression, they also are less likely to attempt suicide. Interestingly, studies have found that the relationship between suicide attempts and religious beliefs isn't significant when controlling for social supports (Rasic et. al, 2009). In other words, the impact that religion has on your sense of social connection might be the biggest benefit.

Coping better with stressful life events

Finally, religious and spiritual people have also been found to cope better with stressful life events. According to one study, people who appraised stressful events through a religious lens (for example, interpreting these events as "part of God's plan") were more likely to psychologically adjust to these events. Seeing the world in this way might also help people feel a sense of control during times when they otherwise feel powerless, like when they've just been through an accident.

This seems to only be true when people attribute stressful life events to God or another higher power. Attributing negative events to the devil (or another negative religious force) actually worsens people's coping and leads to a higher likelihood of developing post-traumatic stress disorder (Ano & Vasconcelles, 2005).

Religion can lead to happiness

If you're a religious person, you may be in luck; your spiritual practice may bring countless benefits to your health and well-being. To reap these benefits, you don't need to join a church. If you don't believe, you can start a spiritual practice simply by reflecting on your role in the universe or starting a meditation practice.

HAPPINESS ACTIVITY 14
WHO AM I?

In the boxes to the left of the page, answer the questions using the words that come to mind when you ask yourself each question. In the boxes to the right, draw an image that flows out of you when pondering these same questions.

Who am I?	Who am I?
Who am I meant to be?	Who am I meant to be?
What needs to come into this world through me?	What needs to come into this world through me?

MINI LESSON 11
SAVORING

What Is Savoring, and How Can It Make You Happier?

THINK ABOUT THE last time you had a truly delicious meal. The food had the perfect flavor and consistency, and every mouthful was a delightful sensory explosion in your mouth.

You may have eaten your meal in minutes. But if the food was *really* delicious, you probably took at least one moment to pay attention to how it tasted. Maybe you tried to enjoy every bite to the fullest. Maybe you even told your dinner companions about how delicious it was.

In other words, you may have *savored* your meal—and that probably made it taste even better.

Positive psychologists say that you can apply this concept of savoring to your happiness, and not just delicious food. When we slow down and really appreciate happy moments, we can maximize the amount of joy we get from them.

What Is Savoring?

Positive psychologist Fred B. Byrant defines the concept of savoring as "the capacit[y] to attend to, appreciate, and enhance the positive experiences in [life]." (Byrant & Veroff, 2007).

Bryant's research has found that people who savor the positive moments in their lives are more likely to be happy. He distinguishes between feeling joy and savoring joy. Many things can bring us joy, but savoring is the active process of paying attention to and enjoying the joy that's present.

How to Savor the Good Times

Positive psychology research states that practicing savoring makes people happier (Jose, Lim, & Bryant, 2012). Savoring also helps you cope better with stressful life events. It can even decrease symptoms of depression (Hurley & Kwon, 2012). People who know how to savor the good times simply enjoy life more. But how can you practice savoring and reap its benefits?

Experts recommend a few different strategies. Next time you find yourself experiencing a happy life event, try one of these techniques to savor the moment and make the happiness last longer Kennelly, 2012).

Behavioral display

Behavioral display is the act of physically showing your emotions. Being demure doesn't help you to savor the moment. Shout your joy from the mountaintops! Clap, laugh, jump up and down—it doesn't matter, as long as you're physically and visibly rejoicing in your happiness.

Sharing with others

Sharing your happy moment with other people is an excellent way to savor the moment. What's got you feeling so happy? Perhaps you've accomplished something at work, or you're just grateful for a good friend's company. Whatever it is, talk about your happy feelings with a loved one. Tell them about your positive event and allow them to share in your joy.

Positive mental time travel

Savoring doesn't have to end when the positive event is in the past. Try practicing positive mental time travel, and actively reminisce about happy memories. Maybe you can watch your wedding video or talk with your friend about the good old days. Whatever you choose to do, try to remember how happy you felt in that moment.

Savoring the good things in life doesn't have to be complicated. When you're happy, make sure you notice you're happy. Enjoy the feeling. It can make all the difference.

HAPPINESS ACTIVITY 15
MINDFUL EATING

This week, you will be practicing mindful eating. Select a meal that you have the time to enjoy. You will need to focus on what you are eating, with no screen interruptions like cell phones, TV or your computer. Cook a meal that you enjoy, take your time, and enjoy the process. Lay out real dishes (if you have grandma's china, this is a good time to use it) and silverware—no paper plates—and plastic spoons. Light a candle and set out a vase of fresh flowers. This is a sensory experience—bask in it. Enjoy each bite of food you take. Taste each component of your dish, down to the seasoning. Each bite should delight your taste buds. Eat slowly, and savor your food.

Write about your experience:

....
....
....
....
....
....
....
....

MINI LESSON 12
VALUES

Using Your Core Values to Increase Happiness

WHAT DO YOU value in life? To some extent, each society values similar things. But you probably have some beliefs, and principles that you value in your life above others. These are your core values, and they often guide your behavior and thinking.

Core values are the fundamental beliefs that define a person or a group. Identifying your core values and intentionally implementing them can lead to a happier, more meaningful life.

Some Values Lead to More Happiness

Living authentically to your values can bring you more meaning and purpose. But one study found that certain values bring more happiness than others. People who valued self-centered things like money, achievement or self-enhancement were less likely to be happy than people who valued self-transcendence and community-oriented things. People who value religion were the most likely to be happy (Lee & Kawatchi, 2019).

This might be something to consider when you're narrowing down your values. What's most important in your life? How can you use these values to increase your happiness?

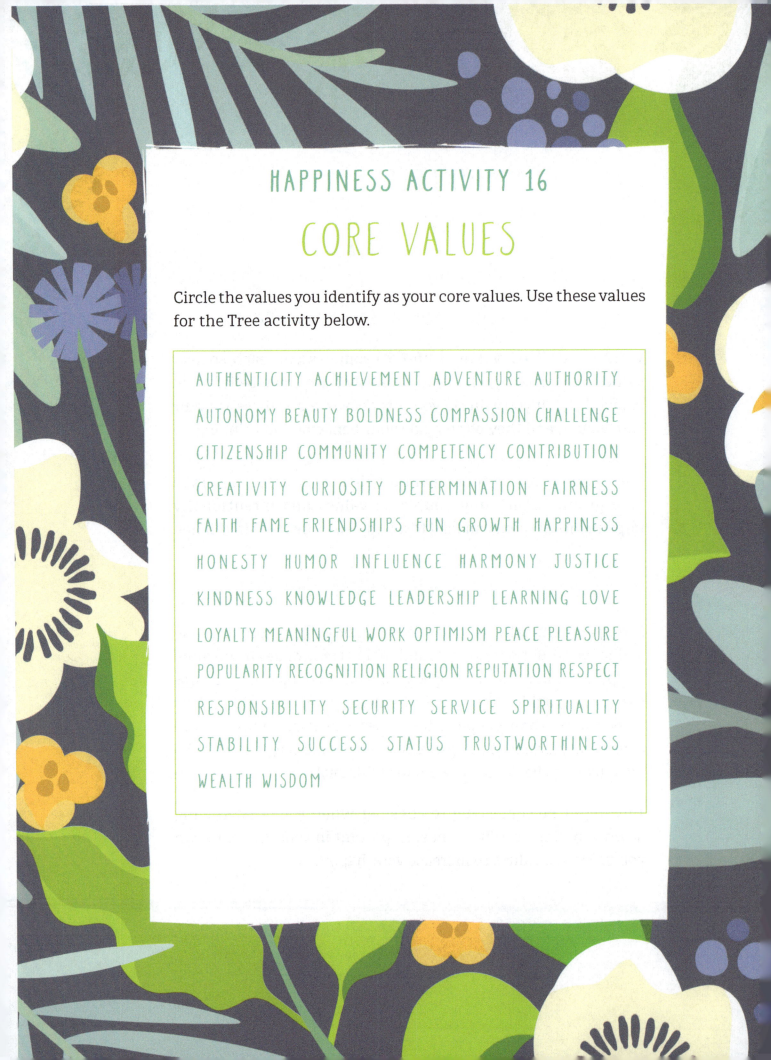

HAPPINESS ACTIVITY 16
CORE VALUES

Circle the values you identify as your core values. Use these values for the Tree activity below.

AUTHENTICITY   ACHIEVEMENT   ADVENTURE   AUTHORITY
AUTONOMY   BEAUTY   BOLDNESS   COMPASSION   CHALLENGE
CITIZENSHIP   COMMUNITY   COMPETENCY   CONTRIBUTION
CREATIVITY   CURIOSITY   DETERMINATION   FAIRNESS
FAITH   FAME   FRIENDSHIPS   FUN   GROWTH   HAPPINESS
HONESTY   HUMOR   INFLUENCE   HARMONY   JUSTICE
KINDNESS   KNOWLEDGE   LEADERSHIP   LEARNING   LOVE
LOYALTY   MEANINGFUL WORK   OPTIMISM   PEACE   PLEASURE
POPULARITY   RECOGNITION   RELIGION   REPUTATION   RESPECT
RESPONSIBILITY   SECURITY   SERVICE   SPIRITUALITY
STABILITY   SUCCESS   STATUS   TRUSTWORTHINESS
WEALTH   WISDOM

Fill in the tree graphic with values from the previous page.

VALUES CHOSEN BY YOU

VALUES INFLUENCED BY PEERS & SOCIETY

PARENT/FAMILY VALUES

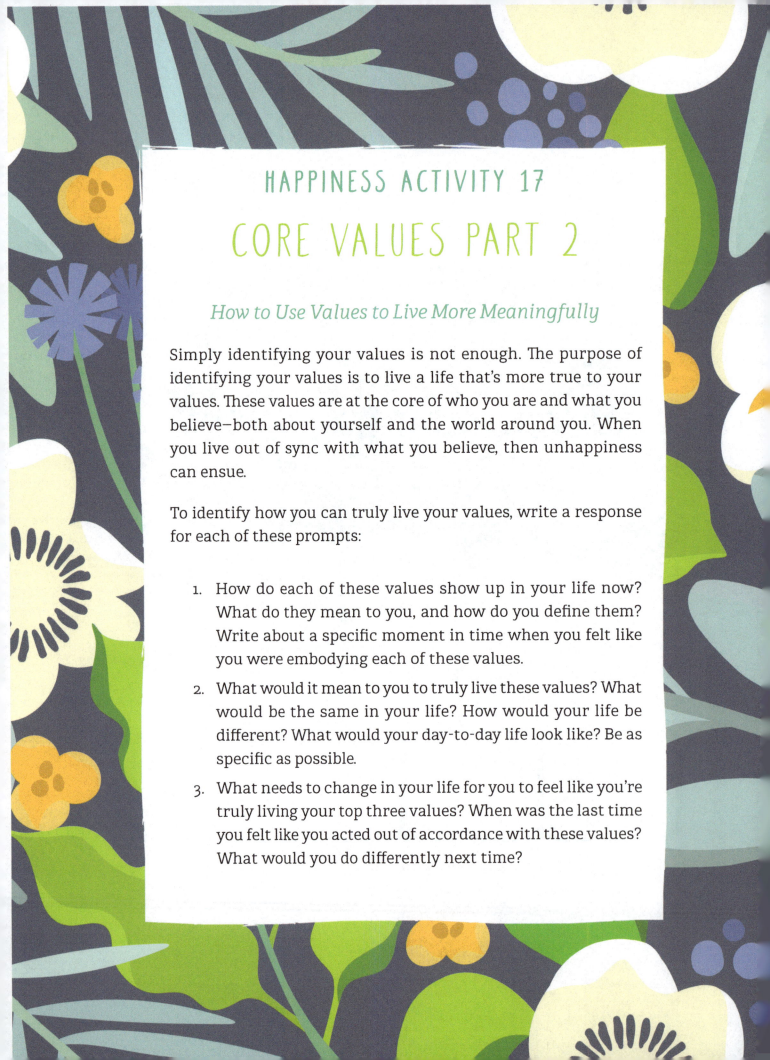

HAPPINESS ACTIVITY 17
CORE VALUES PART 2

How to Use Values to Live More Meaningfully

Simply identifying your values is not enough. The purpose of identifying your values is to live a life that's more true to your values. These values are at the core of who you are and what you believe—both about yourself and the world around you. When you live out of sync with what you believe, then unhappiness can ensue.

To identify how you can truly live your values, write a response for each of these prompts:

1. How do each of these values show up in your life now? What do they mean to you, and how do you define them? Write about a specific moment in time when you felt like you were embodying each of these values.
2. What would it mean to you to truly live these values? What would be the same in your life? How would your life be different? What would your day-to-day life look like? Be as specific as possible.
3. What needs to change in your life for you to feel like you're truly living your top three values? When was the last time you felt like you acted out of accordance with these values? What would you do differently next time?

1. ....

2. ....

3. ....

MINI LESSON 13
SIGNATURE STRENGTHS

What Are Your Strengths and How Can They Help You Lead a Happier Life?

WE USUALLY THINK about our personal strengths as helping us with things like our self-esteem and confidence. But positive psychology researchers have found that knowing your character strengths can actually make you a happier person overall. They've even created an assessment to help you figure out what your strengths are if you're not sure.

The VIA Questionnaire to Find Your Strengths

Some people, when they're asked what their character strengths are, can tell you right away. Others have a harder time answering this question. They might not be aware of what strengths they have to lean on.

If you find yourself in this second group, there is a survey that may help you to identify your most valuable strengths. It's called the Values in Action Survey, or the VIA Survey of Character Strengths. It consists of 240 questions, and respondents must rate each item on a Likert scale. Your answers give insight into what your main character strengths might be (Peter, Christopher & Seligman, 2004).

How to Use Your Strengths for Happiness

Your strengths can get through hard times. They're also important in performing acts of kindness for other people. Dr. Martin E.P. Seligman, one of the leading psychologists at the VIA Institute on Character, wrote that when people performed acts of kindness that utilized their character strengths, they reported greater levels of happiness and life satisfaction.

"When our philanthropic acts were spontaneous and called upon personal strengths, the whole day went better," he said of an experiment he conducted. He added, "The exercise of kindness is a gratification, in contrast to a pleasure. As a gratification, it calls on your strengths to rise to an occasion and meet a challenge." (Seligman, 2002).

Everyone Has Signature Strengths

The best thing about character strengths is that we all have them, although they can be very different. Perhaps one person's character strength is the capacity to love and be loved (building relationships), and another's is being responsible and accountable to promises.

As Seligman says, "The good life consists in deriving happiness by using your signature strengths every day in the main realms of living. The meaningful life adds one more component: using these same strengths to forward knowledge, power or goodness." (Seligman, 2002).

HAPPINESS ACTIVITY 18
VIA TEST

Take the VIA Signature Strengths Test (under Engagement Questionnaires at *www.authentichappiness.sas.upenn.edu/testcenter*) (the survey takes about 25 minutes) and rank your top 5 signature strengths. This week, purposely utilize these strengths in your daily life and write about your experiences below.

1. ....
....
....

2. ....
....
....

3. ....
....
....

4. ....
....
....

5. ....
....
....

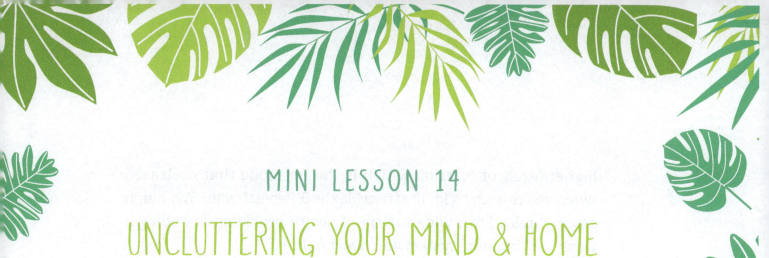

MINI LESSON 14

UNCLUTTERING YOUR MIND & HOME

The Psychological Benefits of Decluttering Your Home

YOU MAY HAVE noticed that when your office or house is messy, you feel stressed. Positive psychologists have conducted research on this phenomenon, and they've found that decluttering your space comes with enormous benefits to your mental health and happiness.

What's Wrong with Clutter?

First, what does it mean to declutter your home, and why is it so important? When we talk about "decluttering," we are referring to the act of getting rid of unnecessary mess. So many of us accumulate stuff in our lives; this can mean both physical "stuff" and mental "stuff." This messy, unorganized "stuff" is what we refer to as clutter.

When we're surrounded by clutter, we can start to feel like everything is out of control. Scientists have found that seeing clutter around you day after day can actually start to become a physical drain on your brain. The human brain needs a certain level of organization. Clutter, for obvious reasons, gives your brain signals of disorganization and chaos. This can distract your brain as it tries to make sense of the mess around you, and can decrease the amount of cognitive resources you have available for other tasks (Gaspar, et. al, 2016).

Clutter can also increase your levels of anxiety and stress. Research has found that people who are surrounded by clutter may have higher levels of cortisol, which is the hormone that's released when you're under a lot of stress (Saxbe & Repetti, 2010). Too much stress can lead to a wide variety of health problems, including a weakened immune system and heart failure.

Other consequences of a cluttered space include suffering relationships, poor eating choices, and lower overall well-being (Roster, Ferrari, & Jurkat, 2016).

The Benefits of Decluttering, and How to Do It

Decluttering your space and home can have enormous mental health benefits, psychologists say. Not only does a decluttered space lead to less cortisol and stress, but it also can result in improved concentration, a happier mood, and better relationships. But how do you start decluttering when you've been living with so much mess all around you?

Marie Kondo, a Japanese organization expert, suggests you start by figuring out what things in your life "spark joy" for you (Kondo & Hirano, 2014). When you pick an item up, how do you feel? There is no need to keep things around that no longer make you feel happy. Thank the item for the ways in which it has served you up until now, and let it go.

Declutter Your Home to Declutter Your Mind

Perhaps the most important psychological benefit to decluttering the space around you is that your mind can end up feeling decluttered, too. As the author of The Artist's Way, Julia Cameron, writes: "When we clear our space, we clear room for new ideas. We make room for insight. We literally clear our minds" (Cameron, 2017).

HAPPINESS ACTIVITY 19

EMPTY YOUR BRAIN JOURNAL

Every morning for the next week, write non-stop until the end of the page. Do not over think about what you are writing; allow anything and everything that wants to come out onto the page to come out. If you get stuck, you can write, "I'm stuck" until something comes to you. The goal of this activity is to get all the heavy thoughts out of your mind, to leave room for more amazing thoughts to settle in.

Empty Your Brain Journal

Day 1

.... All Done!

Empty Your Brain Journal

Day 2

....All Done!

Empty Your Brain Journal

Day 3

....
....
....
....
....
....
....
....
....
....
....
....
....
....
....
....
....
.... All Done!

Empty Your Brain Journal

Day 4

.... All Done!

Empty Your Brain Journal

Day 5

.... All Done!

Empty Your Brain Journal

Day 6

....
....
....
....
....
....
....
....
....
....
....
....
....
....
....
....
....
.... All Done!

Empty Your Brain Journal

Day 7

.... All Done!

HAPPINESS ACTIVITY 20
ORGANIZE YOUR SPACE

"The best way to choose what to keep and what to throw away is to take each item in one's hand and ask: 'Does this spark joy?' If it does, keep it. If not, dispose of it. This is not only the simplest but also the most accurate yardstick by which to judge." —Marie Kondo

Select a room in your home that you spend a good amount of time in and that is need of organization. Organize this space using Marie Kondo's signature, "Does this spark joy?" technique. First, set up three piles; items that need to be thrown out, items to donate, and the items you want to keep. When deciding if you are going to keep an item, ask yourself, does this item still spark joy for me, if it does, keep it, if not, decide if it's worth donating or if it needs to be thrown away. How do you feel now that your room has been decluttered? Write about your experience below.

ROOM: ....

WRITE ABOUT YOUR EXPERIENCE:
....
....
....
....

"Putting your house in order is the magic that creates a vibrant and happy life." —Marie Kondo

MINI LESSON 15
AWE & WONDER

How Can Awe and Wonder Lead to a Happier Life?

WE ALL KNOW the feeling, even though it's hard to describe in words. Maybe you felt it when you heard a symphonic orchestra play for the first time. Maybe you grew up in a city, and it was when you went out into the countryside and saw the milky way in its full glory. Maybe you feel it when you walk into a temple or a cathedral. Or maybe, for you, there was nothing more awe-inspiring than the moment you held your newborn for the first time.

Positive psychologists call this feeling awe, and they've been studying it for years. It's that feeling of goosebump-inducing amazement that we feel, usually when we realize how vast the world actually is. Awe-inducing experiences usually challenge the way we've always thought about the world. Maybe we thought our individual life and problems were the center of the universe, for example, until we saw how many stars are in the galaxy.

Benefits of Awe

Scientists think that feeling awe improves our health because it gets us out of our individualistic minds. Awe-inspiring experiences—like looking out at the vast ocean, for example—help us to transcend the "I" and connect to the "we." It's a collective emotional experience. Awe makes us feel small and insignificant—in a good way (Piff et. al, 2015).

Positive psychologists have studied the scientific benefits of awe. They've found that feeling awe has many benefits for our lives, including:

- Making us more generous (Piff, et. al, 2015)
- Improving our immune system (Stellar, et. al, 2015)
- Less inflammation in the body
- Greater life satisfaction
- Less stress (Anderson, Monroy, & Keltner, 2016)
- Making us better at scientific learning and critical thinking (Griskevicius)
- Making us more humble (Stellar, et. al, 2018).

How to Feel More Awe

Although connecting with the vast natural world is a great way to get more awe into your life, you don't need to fly to the Grand Canyon to get the health benefits. Try to intentionally seek out awe-inspiring experiences on a regular basis, even in small ways. Studies have found that simply watching videos or reading stories about awe-inspiring places and experiences have health benefits.

The key is to intentionally cultivate and be on the lookout for these opportunities. Watch the people around you and look for interactions that inspire you. Maybe your toddler discovering his curiosity fills you with awe. Maybe it's watching two lovers reunite at the airport. Nature is all around us, too—even in cities.

The point is to get out of our small, individualistic minds and have experiences that remind us that we are a small part of a collective whole. If you can learn to do that on a regular basis, then you'll be on your way to a happier, healthier life.

HAPPINESS ACTIVITY 20
THE AWE EXPERIENCE

People most commonly connect to the emotion of awe through nature and through a feeling of connection with others. This week, seek out an Awe Experience. Write about your experience below.

AWE EXPERIENCE: ....

DESCRIBE YOUR EXPERIENCE AND HOW IT MADE YOU FEEL:
....
....
....
....
....
....
....
....
....
....
....

MINI LESSON 16
LAUGHTER & PLAY

The Importance of Laughter and Play

WHEN YOU THINK about pure joy, what do you imagine? Many of us think of a group of children laughing and playing. And we aren't wrong—laughter and playfulness do bring joy, and actually bring us very real health benefits.

In fact, some psychologists think that laughter and play are key components of a happy life.

The Health Benefits of Laughter

You've probably heard the phrase, "Laughter is the best medicine." It turns out that this is more than just an old wives' tale; it has a basis in science. Laughter and play really do have enormous benefits for your happiness and well-being.

When you're under a lot of stress, your body's sympathetic nervous system gets activated. It releases the stress response, which can be harmful when it's activated over a long period of time. Laughter helps to counteract the negative effects of your sympathetic nervous system. When you laugh, endorphins get released—the chemicals that are responsible for lifting your mood (Yim, 2016). They are what's responsible for the great feeling you get after you laugh.

Positive psychology researchers have found that humor can improve our marital, work, and social lives (Louie, Brooke, & Frates, 2016). The physical and mental health benefits of laughter and play include:

- Decreased symptoms of depression and anxiety
- Less aggression–hostility, and anger (Gelkopf, 2011)
- Higher self-esteem, although self-deprecating humor has been linked to lower self-esteem (McCosker & Moran, 2012)
- More creativity (Ziv, 1976)
- Increased immune system (Bennett & Lengacher, 2009).
- Increased pain tolerance (Perez-Aranda et. al, 2019).

On top of these individual benefits of laughing, shared laughter—or laughing with (not at) someone—can help you like that person more and make you feel closer to them (Kurtz & Algoe, 2017).

HAPPINESS ACTIVITY 22
IT'S TIME TO LAUGH & PLAY

This week, select an activity where you are guaranteed to laugh. You can find a local comedy night, or watch a movie that makes you laugh so hard you cry. You can also hang out with a friend who always has something funny to say. You decide what's going to make you laugh out loud!

Next, select an activity that you consider play. If you play a sport you enjoy, make sure to play this week. If dancing is play for you, go out dancing this week. Play pool with friends or play in the pool—just make sure however you decide to play, it's done for fun!

Write down your Laugh & Play experiences this week.

.... made me laugh this week.

HOW DID IT MAKE YOU FEEL?
....
....

I played .... this week.

HOW DID IT MAKE YOU FEEL?
....
....

MINI LESSON 17
GOALS

Setting Meaningful Goals to Create Happiness

HAVING AND WORKING toward goals is an important part of a meaningful life. At the same time, we often don't think about goal-setting as something that makes us happier. Setting out to achieve goals is satisfying, but effort can be grueling and frustrating as well. However, some psychologists say that there are ways to set and work toward goals that increase our happiness and overall well-being.

What Type of Goals Make Us Happier?

To use goals as a means to achieve happiness, it's important to set the right kinds of goals. Setting the wrong goals for ourselves will only lead to failure, disappointment, and frustration.

When thinking about what type of goals makes us happier, it may be easiest to start by thinking about what type of goals makes us unhappy. If you are a person who doesn't value material goods, for example, then working hard and saving money for a new car probably doesn't feel good for you.

The best type of goal to set is one that is in line with your values—a goal that feels deeply meaningful for you.

The host of the *Greater Good Podcast*, Dacher Keltner, puts it this way: "Setting and then pursuing goals can help us become more motivated and productive and feel less depressed, but not all goals. Only the ones that we really value–that create space for growth." (Keltner, 2021).

The Benefits of Goal-Setting

Research has found that setting, working toward, and achieving goals can all have a big impact on our lives. When we set a meaningful goal for ourselves, we challenge ourselves to think of ways to achieve it. We might even think of innovative solutions or ideas about how to overcome obstacles. In other words, goals increase our sense of self-efficacy.

Goal-setting can also make us feel like we're more in control of our life circumstances and surroundings. One study found that people who felt more in control during the pandemic reported less negative emotions and a greater subjective level of life satisfaction and overall well-being (Zacher & Rudolph, 2021).

How to Set Meaningful Goals

To set goals that will bring your life meaning, purpose, and happiness, make sure they're aligned with your values. What are you intrinsically motivated to accomplish? What is it that you truly want to have in life? What do you want more, or less, of?

Think about your core values. What changes could you make in your life that would help you to live those values the way you want to? What character strengths do you have that would help you get there?

When framing your specific goal, you might like to try the SMART goal method (Doran, 1981). Make sure your goals are:

- Specific
- Measurable
- Attainable
- Realistic
- Time-limited.

Don't go overboard and try to set too many goals at one time. Overwhelming yourself with too many goals is a surefire way to want to give up on all of your goals. And when you're working toward your goals, stay optimistic. Research has shown that people who are optimistic about reaching their goals are more likely to put more effort toward achievement, and they're less likely to feel stressed (Lench, et. al, 2021).

Goal-setting doesn't need to be a stressful and anxiety-provoking thing. Set goals that feel meaningful to you and that will bring you closer to your values. In this way, you can increase your well-being and bring purpose to your life.

HAPPINESS ACTIVITY 23
MY FUTURE SELF

Imagine your best life in the future. Consider all the areas of your life, such as your career, relationships, lifestyle, and health. What would your life look like if all the areas of your life were be exactly as you imagine them? Describe your ideal day from when you first wake up to when you fall asleep. What does a typical day in your best life look like? Give lots of details. And, most importantly, don't limit yourself!

A day in the life of my best future self:

....
....
....
....
....
....
....
....
....

HAPPINESS ACTIVITY 24
GOAL SETTING

Let's break down your best future self into measurable goals.

CAREER GOALS:

1. ....
2. ....
3. ....

Steps to achieve them;

1. ....
2. ....
3. ....

Timeline to achieve these goals: ....

RELATIONSHIP GOALS:

1. ....
2. ....
3. ....

Steps to achieve them;

1. ....
2. ....
3. ....

Timeline to achieve these goals: ....

LIFESTYLE GOALS:

1. ....
2. ....
3. ....

Steps to achieve them;

1. ....
2. ....
3. ....

Timeline to achieve these goals: ....

HEALTH GOALS:

1. ....
2. ....
3. ....

Steps to achieve them;

1. ....
2. ....
3. ....

Timeline to achieve these goals: ....

OTHER GOALS:

1. ....
2. ....
3. ....

Steps to achieve them;

1. ....
2. ....
3. ....

Timeline to achieve these goals: ....

CHEERFUL by DESIGN

52-WEEK WORKBOOK

> *Happiness doesn't just happen to you. You have to work at it.*
>
> —Dalai Lama

WEEK 1

"True life is lived when tiny changes occur."

—Leo Tolstoy

FLOW CHECKER	I Am Thankful For:	Acts of Kindness:
....	1.	1. ....
....	2.	2. ....
....	3.	3. ....
....	4.	4. ....
....	5.	5. ....

PERSONAL GOAL

....

3 Good Things:
1. ....
Why? ....
2. ....
Why? ....
3. ....
Why? ....

Fitness Activities:
1. ....
2. ....
3. ....
4. ....
5. ....

Meditation
- MONDAY ☐
- TUESDAY ☐
- WEDNESDAY ☐
- THURSDAY ☐
- FRIDAY ☐
- SATURDAY ☐
- SUNDAY ☐

Empty Your Brain Journal
- MONDAY ☐
- TUESDAY ☐
- WEDNESDAY ☐
- THURSDAY ☐
- FRIDAY ☐
- SATURDAY ☐
- SUNDAY ☐

WEEK 2

"Peace begins with a smile."

—Mother Teresa

FLOW CHECKER

PERSONAL GOAL

I Am Thankful For:
1.
2.
3.
4.
5.

3 Good Things:
1.
Why?
2.
Why?
3.
Why?

Meditation
- MONDAY ☐
- TUESDAY ☐
- WEDNESDAY ☐
- THURSDAY ☐
- FRIDAY ☐
- SATURDAY ☐
- SUNDAY ☐

Acts of Kindness:
1.
2.
3.
4.
5.

Fitness Activities:
1.
2.
3.
4.
5.

Empty Your Brain Journal
- MONDAY ☐
- TUESDAY ☐
- WEDNESDAY ☐
- THURSDAY ☐
- FRIDAY ☐
- SATURDAY ☐
- SUNDAY ☐

WEEK 3

"No act of kindness, no matter how small, is ever wasted."

—Aesop

FLOW CHECKER

I Am Thankful For:
1.
2.
3.
4.
5.

Acts of Kindness:
1.
2.
3.
4.
5.

PERSONAL GOAL

3 Good Things:
1.
Why?
2.
Why?
3.
Why?

Fitness Activities:
1.
2.
3.
4.
5.

Meditation
- MONDAY ☐
- TUESDAY ☐
- WEDNESDAY ☐
- THURSDAY ☐
- FRIDAY ☐
- SATURDAY ☐
- SUNDAY ☐

Empty Your Brain Journal
- MONDAY ☐
- TUESDAY ☐
- WEDNESDAY ☐
- THURSDAY ☐
- FRIDAY ☐
- SATURDAY ☐
- SUNDAY ☐

WEEK 4

"Wherever you go, no matter what the weather, always bring your own sunshine."

—Anthony J. D'Angelo

FLOW CHECKER

....
....
....
....
....
....
....

I Am Thankful For:

1. ....
2. ....
3. ....
4. ....
5. ....

Acts of Kindness:

1. ....
2. ....
3. ....
4. ....
5. ....

PERSONAL GOAL

....
....
....
....
....
....
....
....
....
....

3 Good Things:

1. ....
Why? ....
2. ....
Why? ....
3. ....
Why? ....

Fitness Activities:

1. ....
2. ....
3. ....
4. ....
5. ....

Meditation

- MONDAY ☐
- TUESDAY ☐
- WEDNESDAY ☐
- THURSDAY ☐
- FRIDAY ☐
- SATURDAY ☐
- SUNDAY ☐

Empty Your Brain Journal

- MONDAY ☐
- TUESDAY ☐
- WEDNESDAY ☐
- THURSDAY ☐
- FRIDAY ☐
- SATURDAY ☐
- SUNDAY ☐

WEEK 5

"Life shrinks or expands in proportion to one's courage."

—Anais Nin

FLOW CHECKER

....
....
....
....
....
....

I Am Thankful For:

1. ....
2. ....
3. ....
4. ....
5. ....

Acts of Kindness:

1. ....
2. ....
3. ....
4. ....
5. ....

PERSONAL GOAL

....
....
....
....
....
....
....
....
....
....
....
....

3 Good Things:

1. ....
Why? ....
2. ....
Why? ....
3. ....
Why? ....

Fitness Activities:

1. ....
2. ....
3. ....
4. ....
5. ....

Meditation

- MONDAY ☐
- TUESDAY ☐
- WEDNESDAY ☐
- THURSDAY ☐
- FRIDAY ☐
- SATURDAY ☐
- SUNDAY ☐

Empty Your Brain Journal

- MONDAY ☐
- TUESDAY ☐
- WEDNESDAY ☐
- THURSDAY ☐
- FRIDAY ☐
- SATURDAY ☐
- SUNDAY ☐

WEEK 6

"I rather have roses on my table than diamonds on my neck."

—Emma Goldman

FLOW CHECKER	I Am Thankful For:	Acts of Kindness:
....	1.	1. ....
....	2.	2. ....
....	3.	3. ....
....	4.	4. ....
....	5.	5. ....

PERSONAL GOAL

3 Good Things:
1. ....
Why? ....
2. ....
Why? ....
3. ....
Why? ....

Fitness Activities:
1. ....
2. ....
3. ....
4. ....
5. ....

Meditation
- MONDAY ☐
- TUESDAY ☐
- WEDNESDAY ☐
- THURSDAY ☐
- FRIDAY ☐
- SATURDAY ☐
- SUNDAY ☐

Empty Your Brain Journal
- MONDAY ☐
- TUESDAY ☐
- WEDNESDAY ☐
- THURSDAY ☐
- FRIDAY ☐
- SATURDAY ☐
- SUNDAY ☐

WEEK 7

"I am born happy every morning."

—**Unknown**

FLOW CHECKER	I Am Thankful For:	Acts of Kindness:
	1.	1.
	2.	2.
	3.	3.
	4.	4.
	5.	5.

PERSONAL GOAL	3 Good Things:	Fitness Activities:
	1. .... Why? .... 2. .... Why? .... 3. .... Why?	1. .... 2. .... 3. .... 4. .... 5. ....

Meditation
- MONDAY ☐
- TUESDAY ☐
- WEDNESDAY ☐
- THURSDAY ☐
- FRIDAY ☐
- SATURDAY ☐
- SUNDAY ☐

Empty Your Brain Journal
- MONDAY ☐
- TUESDAY ☐
- WEDNESDAY ☐
- THURSDAY ☐
- FRIDAY ☐
- SATURDAY ☐
- SUNDAY ☐

WEEK 8

"Man is asked to make of himself what he is supposed to become to fulfill his destiny."

—Paul Tillich

FLOW CHECKER

....
....
....
....
....
....

I Am Thankful For:

1. ....
2. ....
3. ....
4. ....
5. ....

Acts of Kindness:

1. ....
2. ....
3. ....
4. ....
5. ....

PERSONAL GOAL

....
....
....
....
....
....
....
....
....
....

3 Good Things:

1. ....
Why? ....
2. ....
Why? ....
3. ....
Why? ....

Fitness Activities:

1. ....
2. ....
3. ....
4. ....
5. ....

Meditation

- [ ] MONDAY
- [ ] TUESDAY
- [ ] WEDNESDAY
- [ ] THURSDAY
- [ ] FRIDAY
- [ ] SATURDAY
- [ ] SUNDAY

Empty Your Brain Journal

- [ ] MONDAY
- [ ] TUESDAY
- [ ] WEDNESDAY
- [ ] THURSDAY
- [ ] FRIDAY
- [ ] SATURDAY
- [ ] SUNDAY

WEEK 9

"What we play is life."

—Louis Armstrong

FLOW CHECKER

I Am Thankful For:
1.
2.
3.
4.
5.

Acts of Kindness:
1.
2.
3.
4.
5.

PERSONAL GOAL

3 Good Things:
1.
Why?
2.
Why?
3.
Why?

Fitness Activities:
1.
2.
3.
4.
5.

Meditation
- MONDAY ☐
- TUESDAY ☐
- WEDNESDAY ☐
- THURSDAY ☐
- FRIDAY ☐
- SATURDAY ☐
- SUNDAY ☐

Empty Your Brain Journal
- MONDAY ☐
- TUESDAY ☐
- WEDNESDAY ☐
- THURSDAY ☐
- FRIDAY ☐
- SATURDAY ☐
- SUNDAY ☐

WEEK 10

"Money will come when you are doing the right things."

—Mike Phillips

| **FLOW CHECKER** | **I Am Thankful For:** | **Acts of Kindness:** |

1. ....
2. ....
3. ....
4. ....
5. ....

| **PERSONAL GOAL** | **3 Good Things:** | **Fitness Activities:** |

1. ....
Why? ....
2. ....
Why? ....
3. ....
Why? ....

Meditation
- MONDAY ☐
- TUESDAY ☐
- WEDNESDAY ☐
- THURSDAY ☐
- FRIDAY ☐
- SATURDAY ☐
- SUNDAY ☐

Empty Your Brain Journal
- MONDAY ☐
- TUESDAY ☐
- WEDNESDAY ☐
- THURSDAY ☐
- FRIDAY ☐
- SATURDAY ☐
- SUNDAY ☐

WEEK 11

"Explore daily the will of God."

—C.G. Jung

FLOW CHECKER

....
....
....
....
....
....

I Am Thankful For:

1. ....
2. ....
3. ....
4. ....
5. ....

Acts of Kindness:

1. ....
2. ....
3. ....
4. ....
5. ....

PERSONAL GOAL

....
....
....
....
....
....
....
....
....
....
....
....

3 Good Things:

1. ....
Why? ....
2. ....
Why? ....
3. ....
Why? ....

Fitness Activities:

1. ....
2. ....
3. ....
4. ....
5. ....

Meditation

- MONDAY ☐
- TUESDAY ☐
- WEDNESDAY ☐
- THURSDAY ☐
- FRIDAY ☐
- SATURDAY ☐
- SUNDAY ☐

Empty Your Brain Journal

- MONDAY ☐
- TUESDAY ☐
- WEDNESDAY ☐
- THURSDAY ☐
- FRIDAY ☐
- SATURDAY ☐
- SUNDAY ☐

WEEK 12

"Shoot for the moon. Even if you miss it you will land among the stars."

—Les Brown

FLOW CHECKER

....
....
....
....
....
....
....

I Am Thankful For:

1. ....
2. ....
3. ....
4. ....
5. ....

Acts of Kindness:

1. ....
2. ....
3. ....
4. ....
5. ....

PERSONAL GOAL

....
....
....
....
....
....
....
....
....
....
....
....
....

3 Good Things:

1. ....
Why? ....
2. ....
Why? ....
3. ....
Why? ....

Fitness Activities:

1. ....
2. ....
3. ....
4. ....
5. ....

Meditation

- MONDAY ☐
- TUESDAY ☐
- WEDNESDAY ☐
- THURSDAY ☐
- FRIDAY ☐
- SATURDAY ☐
- SUNDAY ☐

Empty Your Brain Journal

- MONDAY ☐
- TUESDAY ☐
- WEDNESDAY ☐
- THURSDAY ☐
- FRIDAY ☐
- SATURDAY ☐
- SUNDAY ☐

WEEK 13

"Imagination is more important than knowledge."

—**Albert Einstein**

FLOW CHECKER

I Am Thankful For:
1. ....
2. ....
3. ....
4. ....
5. ....

Acts of Kindness:
1. ....
2. ....
3. ....
4. ....
5. ....

PERSONAL GOAL

3 Good Things:
1. ....
Why? ....
2. ....
Why? ....
3. ....
Why? ....

Fitness Activities:
1. ....
2. ....
3. ....
4. ....
5. ....

Meditation
- MONDAY ☐
- TUESDAY ☐
- WEDNESDAY ☐
- THURSDAY ☐
- FRIDAY ☐
- SATURDAY ☐
- SUNDAY ☐

Empty Your Brain Journal
- MONDAY ☐
- TUESDAY ☐
- WEDNESDAY ☐
- THURSDAY ☐
- FRIDAY ☐
- SATURDAY ☐
- SUNDAY ☐

WEEK 14

"Taking a new step, uttering a new word is what people fear most."

—Fyodor Dostoyevski

FLOW CHECKER

I Am Thankful For:
1.
2.
3.
4.
5.

Acts of Kindness:
1.
2.
3.
4.
5.

PERSONAL GOAL

3 Good Things:
1.
Why?
2.
Why?
3.
Why?

Fitness Activities:
1.
2.
3.
4.
5.

Meditation
- MONDAY ☐
- TUESDAY ☐
- WEDNESDAY ☐
- THURSDAY ☐
- FRIDAY ☐
- SATURDAY ☐
- SUNDAY ☐

Empty Your Brain Journal
- MONDAY ☐
- TUESDAY ☐
- WEDNESDAY ☐
- THURSDAY ☐
- FRIDAY ☐
- SATURDAY ☐
- SUNDAY ☐

WEEK 15

"We learn to do something by doing it. There is no other way."

—John Holt

FLOW CHECKER	I Am Thankful For:	Acts of Kindness:
	1.	1.
	2.	2.
	3.	3.
	4.	4.
	5.	5.

PERSONAL GOAL	3 Good Things:	Fitness Activities:
	1. .... Why?	1.
	2. .... Why?	2.
		3.
	3. .... Why?	4.
		5.

Meditation
- MONDAY ☐
- TUESDAY ☐
- WEDNESDAY ☐
- THURSDAY ☐
- FRIDAY ☐
- SATURDAY ☐
- SUNDAY ☐

Empty Your Brain Journal
- MONDAY ☐
- TUESDAY ☐
- WEDNESDAY ☐
- THURSDAY ☐
- FRIDAY ☐
- SATURDAY ☐
- SUNDAY ☐

WEEK 16

"In the middle of difficulty lies opportunity."

—Albert Einstein

FLOW CHECKER	I Am Thankful For:	Acts of Kindness:
	1.	1.
	2.	2.
	3.	3.
	4.	4.
	5.	5.

PERSONAL GOAL	3 Good Things:	Fitness Activities:
	1. Why? 2. Why? 3. Why?	1. 2. 3. 4. 5.

Meditation
- MONDAY ☐
- TUESDAY ☐
- WEDNESDAY ☐
- THURSDAY ☐
- FRIDAY ☐
- SATURDAY ☐
- SUNDAY ☐

Empty Your Brain Journal
- MONDAY ☐
- TUESDAY ☐
- WEDNESDAY ☐
- THURSDAY ☐
- FRIDAY ☐
- SATURDAY ☐
- SUNDAY ☐

WEEK 17

"Adventures don't begin until you get into the forest. That first step in an act of faith."

—Mickey Heart

FLOW CHECKER

I Am Thankful For:
1.
2.
3.
4.
5.

Acts of Kindness:
1.
2.
3.
4.
5.

PERSONAL GOAL

3 Good Things:
1.
Why?
2.
Why?
3.
Why?

Fitness Activities:
1.
2.
3.
4.
5.

Meditation
- MONDAY ☐
- TUESDAY ☐
- WEDNESDAY ☐
- THURSDAY ☐
- FRIDAY ☐
- SATURDAY ☐
- SUNDAY ☐

Empty Your Brain Journal
- MONDAY ☐
- TUESDAY ☐
- WEDNESDAY ☐
- THURSDAY ☐
- FRIDAY ☐
- SATURDAY ☐
- SUNDAY ☐

WEEK 18

"Keeping baggage from the past will leave no room for happiness in the future."

—Wayne L. Misner

FLOW CHECKER

....
....
....
....
....
....

I Am Thankful For:

1. ....
2. ....
3. ....
4. ....
5. ....

Acts of Kindness:

1. ....
2. ....
3. ....
4. ....
5. ....

PERSONAL GOAL

....
....
....
....
....
....
....
....
....
....

3 Good Things:

1. ....
Why? ....
2. ....
Why? ....
3. ....
Why? ....

Fitness Activities:

1. ....
2. ....
3. ....
4. ....
5. ....

Meditation

- MONDAY ☐
- TUESDAY ☐
- WEDNESDAY ☐
- THURSDAY ☐
- FRIDAY ☐
- SATURDAY ☐
- SUNDAY ☐

Empty Your Brain Journal

- MONDAY ☐
- TUESDAY ☐
- WEDNESDAY ☐
- THURSDAY ☐
- FRIDAY ☐
- SATURDAY ☐
- SUNDAY ☐

WEEK 19

"An early-morning walk is a blessing for the whole day."

–Henry David Thoreau

FLOW CHECKER	I Am Thankful For:	Acts of Kindness:
	1.	1.
	2.	2.
	3.	3.
	4.	4.
	5.	5.

PERSONAL GOAL	3 Good Things:	Fitness Activities:
	1. .... Why? .... 2. .... Why? .... 3. .... Why?	1. 2. 3. 4. 5.

Meditation
- [ ] MONDAY
- [ ] TUESDAY
- [ ] WEDNESDAY
- [ ] THURSDAY
- [ ] FRIDAY
- [ ] SATURDAY
- [ ] SUNDAY

Empty Your Brain Journal
- [ ] MONDAY
- [ ] TUESDAY
- [ ] WEDNESDAY
- [ ] THURSDAY
- [ ] FRIDAY
- [ ] SATURDAY
- [ ] SUNDAY

WEEK 20

"May you always walk in sunshine. May you never want for more."
—Irish Blessing

FLOW CHECKER
....
....
....
....
....
....

I Am Thankful For:
1. ....
2. ....
3. ....
4. ....
5. ....

Acts of Kindness:
1. ....
2. ....
3. ....
4. ....
5. ....

PERSONAL GOAL
....
....
....
....
....
....
....
....
....
....
....

3 Good Things:
1. ....
Why? ....
2. ....
Why? ....
3. ....
Why? ....

Fitness Activities:
1. ....
2. ....
3. ....
4. ....
5. ....

Meditation
- MONDAY ☐
- TUESDAY ☐
- WEDNESDAY ☐
- THURSDAY ☐
- FRIDAY ☐
- SATURDAY ☐
- SUNDAY ☐

Empty Your Brain Journal
- MONDAY ☐
- TUESDAY ☐
- WEDNESDAY ☐
- THURSDAY ☐
- FRIDAY ☐
- SATURDAY ☐
- SUNDAY ☐

WEEK 21

*"Find a way to be thankful for your troubles,
and they can become your blessings."*

—Unknown

FLOW CHECKER

....
....
....
....
....
....
....

I Am Thankful For:

1. ....
2. ....
3. ....
4. ....
5. ....

Acts of Kindness:

1. ....
2. ....
3. ....
4. ....
5. ....

PERSONAL GOAL

....
....
....
....
....
....
....
....
....
....
....
....
....
....

3 Good Things:

1. ....
Why? ....
2. ....
Why? ....
3. ....
Why? ....

Fitness Activities:

1. ....
2. ....
3. ....
4. ....
5. ....

Meditation

- MONDAY ☐
- TUESDAY ☐
- WEDNESDAY ☐
- THURSDAY ☐
- FRIDAY ☐
- SATURDAY ☐
- SUNDAY ☐

Empty Your Brain Journal

- MONDAY ☐
- TUESDAY ☐
- WEDNESDAY ☐
- THURSDAY ☐
- FRIDAY ☐
- SATURDAY ☐
- SUNDAY ☐

WEEK 22

"Humor is mankind's greatest blessing."

–Mark Twain

FLOW CHECKER

....
....
....
....
....
....

PERSONAL GOAL

....
....
....
....
....
....
....
....
....
....
....

I Am Thankful For:
1. ....
2. ....
3. ....
4. ....
5. ....

3 Good Things:
1. ....
Why? ....
2. ....
Why? ....
3. ....
Why? ....

Meditation
- MONDAY ☐
- TUESDAY ☐
- WEDNESDAY ☐
- THURSDAY ☐
- FRIDAY ☐
- SATURDAY ☐
- SUNDAY ☐

Acts of Kindness:
1. ....
2. ....
3. ....
4. ....
5. ....

Fitness Activities:
1. ....
2. ....
3. ....
4. ....
5. ....

Empty Your Brain Journal
- MONDAY ☐
- TUESDAY ☐
- WEDNESDAY ☐
- THURSDAY ☐
- FRIDAY ☐
- SATURDAY ☐
- SUNDAY ☐

WEEK 23

"Joy is not in things: it is in us."

—Richard Wagner

FLOW CHECKER

I Am Thankful For:
1.
2.
3.
4.
5.

Acts of Kindness:
1.
2.
3.
4.
5.

PERSONAL GOAL

3 Good Things:
1.
Why?
2.
Why?
3.
Why?

Fitness Activities:
1.
2.
3.
4.
5.

Meditation
- MONDAY ☐
- TUESDAY ☐
- WEDNESDAY ☐
- THURSDAY ☐
- FRIDAY ☐
- SATURDAY ☐
- SUNDAY ☐

Empty Your Brain Journal
- MONDAY ☐
- TUESDAY ☐
- WEDNESDAY ☐
- THURSDAY ☐
- FRIDAY ☐
- SATURDAY ☐
- SUNDAY ☐

WEEK 24

"A contented mind is the greatest blessing a man can enjoy in this world."

—Joseph Addison

FLOW CHECKER

....
....
....
....
....
....

PERSONAL GOAL

....
....
....
....
....
....
....
....
....
....
....
....

I Am Thankful For:

1. ....
2. ....
3. ....
4. ....
5. ....

3 Good Things:

1. ....
Why? ....
2. ....
Why? ....
3. ....
Why? ....

Acts of Kindness:

1. ....
2. ....
3. ....
4. ....
5. ....

Fitness Activities:

1. ....
2. ....
3. ....
4. ....
5. ....

Meditation

- MONDAY ☐
- TUESDAY ☐
- WEDNESDAY ☐
- THURSDAY ☐
- FRIDAY ☐
- SATURDAY ☐
- SUNDAY ☐

Empty Your Brain Journal

- MONDAY ☐
- TUESDAY ☐
- WEDNESDAY ☐
- THURSDAY ☐
- FRIDAY ☐
- SATURDAY ☐
- SUNDAY ☐

WEEK 25

"Sometimes the best gain is to lose."

—George Herbert

FLOW CHECKER

I Am Thankful For:
1.
2.
3.
4.
5.

Acts of Kindness:
1.
2.
3.
4.
5.

PERSONAL GOAL

3 Good Things:
1.
Why?
2.
Why?
3.
Why?

Fitness Activities:
1.
2.
3.
4.
5.

Meditation
MONDAY ☐
TUESDAY ☐
WEDNESDAY ☐
THURSDAY ☐
FRIDAY ☐
SATURDAY ☐
SUNDAY ☐

Empty Your Brain Journal
MONDAY ☐
TUESDAY ☐
WEDNESDAY ☐
THURSDAY ☐
FRIDAY ☐
SATURDAY ☐
SUNDAY ☐

WEEK 26

"The small happy moments add up. A little bit of joy goes a long way."

—Melissa McCarthy

FLOW CHECKER

PERSONAL GOAL

I Am Thankful For:
1.
2.
3.
4.
5.

3 Good Things:
1.
Why?
2.
Why?
3.
Why?

Acts of Kindness:
1.
2.
3.
4.
5.

Fitness Activities:
1.
2.
3.
4.
5.

Meditation
- MONDAY ☐
- TUESDAY ☐
- WEDNESDAY ☐
- THURSDAY ☐
- FRIDAY ☐
- SATURDAY ☐
- SUNDAY ☐

Empty Your Brain Journal
- MONDAY ☐
- TUESDAY ☐
- WEDNESDAY ☐
- THURSDAY ☐
- FRIDAY ☐
- SATURDAY ☐
- SUNDAY ☐

WEEK 27

"Enjoy the little things, for one day you may look back and realize they were the big things."

—Robert Brault

FLOW CHECKER	I Am Thankful For:	Acts of Kindness:
	1.	1.
	2.	2.
	3.	3.
	4.	4.
	5.	5.

PERSONAL GOAL	3 Good Things:	Fitness Activities:
	1. .... Why? .... 2. .... Why? .... 3. .... Why?	1. 2. 3. 4. 5.

Meditation
- ☐ MONDAY
- ☐ TUESDAY
- ☐ WEDNESDAY
- ☐ THURSDAY
- ☐ FRIDAY
- ☐ SATURDAY
- ☐ SUNDAY

Empty Your Brain Journal
- ☐ MONDAY
- ☐ TUESDAY
- ☐ WEDNESDAY
- ☐ THURSDAY
- ☐ FRIDAY
- ☐ SATURDAY
- ☐ SUNDAY

WEEK 28

"The art of being happy lies in the power of extracting happiness from common things."

—Henry Ward Beecher

FLOW CHECKER	I Am Thankful For:	Acts of Kindness:

1. ....
2. ....
3. ....
4. ....
5. ....

PERSONAL GOAL	3 Good Things:	Fitness Activities:

1. ....
Why? ....
2. ....
Why? ....
3. ....
Why? ....

Meditation
- MONDAY ☐
- TUESDAY ☐
- WEDNESDAY ☐
- THURSDAY ☐
- FRIDAY ☐
- SATURDAY ☐
- SUNDAY ☐

Empty Your Brain Journal
- MONDAY ☐
- TUESDAY ☐
- WEDNESDAY ☐
- THURSDAY ☐
- FRIDAY ☐
- SATURDAY ☐
- SUNDAY ☐

WEEK 29

"The most simple things can bring the most happiness."

—Izabella Scorupco

FLOW CHECKER	I Am Thankful For:	Acts of Kindness:
....	1.	1. ....
....	2.	2. ....
....	3.	3. ....
....	4.	4. ....
....	5.	5. ....

PERSONAL GOAL

....

3 Good Things:

1. ....
Why? ....
2. ....
Why? ....
3. ....
Why? ....

Fitness Activities:

1. ....
2. ....
3. ....
4. ....
5. ....

Meditation

- MONDAY ☐
- TUESDAY ☐
- WEDNESDAY ☐
- THURSDAY ☐
- FRIDAY ☐
- SATURDAY ☐
- SUNDAY ☐

Empty Your Brain Journal

- MONDAY ☐
- TUESDAY ☐
- WEDNESDAY ☐
- THURSDAY ☐
- FRIDAY ☐
- SATURDAY ☐
- SUNDAY ☐

WEEK 30

"Things turn out best for people who make the best of the way things turn out."

—John Wooden

FLOW CHECKER

I Am Thankful For:
1.
2.
3.
4.
5.

Acts of Kindness:
1.
2.
3.
4.
5.

PERSONAL GOAL

3 Good Things:
1.
Why?
2.
Why?
3.
Why?

Fitness Activities:
1.
2.
3.
4.
5.

Meditation
- MONDAY ☐
- TUESDAY ☐
- WEDNESDAY ☐
- THURSDAY ☐
- FRIDAY ☐
- SATURDAY ☐
- SUNDAY ☐

Empty Your Brain Journal
- MONDAY ☐
- TUESDAY ☐
- WEDNESDAY ☐
- THURSDAY ☐
- FRIDAY ☐
- SATURDAY ☐
- SUNDAY ☐

WEEK 31

"Spread love everywhere you go. Let no one ever come to you without leaving happier."

—Mother Teresa

FLOW CHECKER

I Am Thankful For:
1.
2.
3.
4.
5.

Acts of Kindness:
1.
2.
3.
4.
5.

PERSONAL GOAL

3 Good Things:
1.
Why?
2.
Why?
3.
Why?

Fitness Activities:
1.
2.
3.
4.
5.

Meditation
- MONDAY ☐
- TUESDAY ☐
- WEDNESDAY ☐
- THURSDAY ☐
- FRIDAY ☐
- SATURDAY ☐
- SUNDAY ☐

Empty Your Brain Journal
- MONDAY ☐
- TUESDAY ☐
- WEDNESDAY ☐
- THURSDAY ☐
- FRIDAY ☐
- SATURDAY ☐
- SUNDAY ☐

WEEK 32

"Start by doing what's necessary; then do what's possible; and suddenly you are doing the impossible."

—Francis of Assisi

FLOW CHECKER

....
....
....
....
....

I Am Thankful For:

1. ....
2. ....
3. ....
4. ....
5. ....

Acts of Kindness:

1. ....
2. ....
3. ....
4. ....
5. ....

PERSONAL GOAL

....
....
....
....
....
....
....
....
....
....
....
....
....

3 Good Things:

1. ....
Why? ....
2. ....
Why? ....
3. ....
Why? ....

Fitness Activities:

1. ....
2. ....
3. ....
4. ....
5. ....

Meditation

- MONDAY ☐
- TUESDAY ☐
- WEDNESDAY ☐
- THURSDAY ☐
- FRIDAY ☐
- SATURDAY ☐
- SUNDAY ☐

Empty Your Brain Journal

- MONDAY ☐
- TUESDAY ☐
- WEDNESDAY ☐
- THURSDAY ☐
- FRIDAY ☐
- SATURDAY ☐
- SUNDAY ☐

WEEK 33

"Just one small positive thought in the morning can change your whole day."

–Dalai Lama

FLOW CHECKER

I Am Thankful For:
1.
2.
3.
4.
5.

Acts of Kindness:
1.
2.
3.
4.
5.

PERSONAL GOAL

3 Good Things:
1.
Why?
2.
Why?
3.
Why?

Fitness Activities:
1.
2.
3.
4.
5.

Meditation
- MONDAY ☐
- TUESDAY ☐
- WEDNESDAY ☐
- THURSDAY ☐
- FRIDAY ☐
- SATURDAY ☐
- SUNDAY ☐

Empty Your Brain Journal
- MONDAY ☐
- TUESDAY ☐
- WEDNESDAY ☐
- THURSDAY ☐
- FRIDAY ☐
- SATURDAY ☐
- SUNDAY ☐

WEEK 34

"Where there is charity and wisdom, there is neither fear nor ignorance."

—Francis of Assisi

FLOW CHECKER

I Am Thankful For:
1.
2.
3.
4.
5.

Acts of Kindness:
1.
2.
3.
4.
5.

PERSONAL GOAL

3 Good Things:
1.
Why?
2.
Why?
3.
Why?

Fitness Activities:
1.
2.
3.
4.
5.

Meditation
- MONDAY ☐
- TUESDAY ☐
- WEDNESDAY ☐
- THURSDAY ☐
- FRIDAY ☐
- SATURDAY ☐
- SUNDAY ☐

Empty Your Brain Journal
- MONDAY ☐
- TUESDAY ☐
- WEDNESDAY ☐
- THURSDAY ☐
- FRIDAY ☐
- SATURDAY ☐
- SUNDAY ☐

WEEK 35

"Together we can change the world, just one random act of kindness at a time."

–Ron Hall

FLOW CHECKER	I Am Thankful For:	Acts of Kindness:

1. ....
2. ....
3. ....
4. ....
5. ....

PERSONAL GOAL

3 Good Things:
1. ....
Why? ....
2. ....
Why? ....
3. ....
Why? ....

Fitness Activities:
1. ....
2. ....
3. ....
4. ....
5. ....

Meditation
- MONDAY ☐
- TUESDAY ☐
- WEDNESDAY ☐
- THURSDAY ☐
- FRIDAY ☐
- SATURDAY ☐
- SUNDAY ☐

Empty Your Brain Journal
- MONDAY ☐
- TUESDAY ☐
- WEDNESDAY ☐
- THURSDAY ☐
- FRIDAY ☐
- SATURDAY ☐
- SUNDAY ☐

WEEK 36

"Just imagine how different the world could be if we all spoke to everyone with respect and kindness."

—Holly Branson

FLOW CHECKER

I Am Thankful For:
1.
2.
3.
4.
5.

Acts of Kindness:
1.
2.
3.
4.
5.

PERSONAL GOAL

3 Good Things:
1.
Why?
2.
Why?
3.
Why?

Fitness Activities:
1.
2.
3.
4.
5.

Meditation
- MONDAY ☐
- TUESDAY ☐
- WEDNESDAY ☐
- THURSDAY ☐
- FRIDAY ☐
- SATURDAY ☐
- SUNDAY ☐

Empty Your Brain Journal
- MONDAY ☐
- TUESDAY ☐
- WEDNESDAY ☐
- THURSDAY ☐
- FRIDAY ☐
- SATURDAY ☐
- SUNDAY ☐

WEEK 37

"Wherever there is a human being, there is an opportunity for a kindness."

—Lucius Annaeus Seneca

FLOW CHECKER

....
....
....
....
....
....
....

I Am Thankful For:

1. ....
2. ....
3. ....
4. ....
5. ....

Acts of Kindness:

1. ....
2. ....
3. ....
4. ....
5. ....

PERSONAL GOAL

....
....
....
....
....
....
....
....
....
....
....
....
....

3 Good Things:

1. ....
Why? ....
2. ....
Why? ....
3. ....
Why? ....

Fitness Activities:

1. ....
2. ....
3. ....
4. ....
5. ....

Meditation

- MONDAY ☐
- TUESDAY ☐
- WEDNESDAY ☐
- THURSDAY ☐
- FRIDAY ☐
- SATURDAY ☐
- SUNDAY ☐

Empty Your Brain Journal

- MONDAY ☐
- TUESDAY ☐
- WEDNESDAY ☐
- THURSDAY ☐
- FRIDAY ☐
- SATURDAY ☐
- SUNDAY ☐

WEEK 38

"A warm smile is the universal language of kindness."

—William Arthur Ward

FLOW CHECKER

....
....
....
....
....
....
....

I Am Thankful For:

1. ....
2. ....
3. ....
4. ....
5. ....

Acts of Kindness:

1. ....
2. ....
3. ....
4. ....
5. ....

PERSONAL GOAL

....
....
....
....
....
....
....
....
....
....
....
....

3 Good Things:

1. ....
Why? ....
2. ....
Why? ....
3. ....
Why? ....

Fitness Activities:

1. ....
2. ....
3. ....
4. ....
5. ....

Meditation

- MONDAY ☐
- TUESDAY ☐
- WEDNESDAY ☐
- THURSDAY ☐
- FRIDAY ☐
- SATURDAY ☐
- SUNDAY ☐

Empty Your Brain Journal

- MONDAY ☐
- TUESDAY ☐
- WEDNESDAY ☐
- THURSDAY ☐
- FRIDAY ☐
- SATURDAY ☐
- SUNDAY ☐

WEEK 39

"There is nothing in a caterpillar that tells you it's going to be a butterfly."

—R. Buckminster Fuller

FLOW CHECKER

....
....
....
....
....
....

I Am Thankful For:

1. ....
2. ....
3. ....
4. ....
5. ....

Acts of Kindness:

1. ....
2. ....
3. ....
4. ....
5. ....

PERSONAL GOAL

....
....
....
....
....
....
....
....
....
....
....
....

3 Good Things:

1. ....
Why? ....
2. ....
Why? ....
3. ....
Why? ....

Fitness Activities:

1. ....
2. ....
3. ....
4. ....
5. ....

Meditation

- MONDAY ☐
- TUESDAY ☐
- WEDNESDAY ☐
- THURSDAY ☐
- FRIDAY ☐
- SATURDAY ☐
- SUNDAY ☐

Empty Your Brain Journal

- MONDAY ☐
- TUESDAY ☐
- WEDNESDAY ☐
- THURSDAY ☐
- FRIDAY ☐
- SATURDAY ☐
- SUNDAY ☐

WEEK 40

"The good life is a process, not a state of being."

—Carl Rogers

FLOW CHECKER	I Am Thankful For:	Acts of Kindness:
	1.	1.
	2.	2.
	3.	3.
	4.	4.
	5.	5.

PERSONAL GOAL	3 Good Things:	Fitness Activities:
	1. .... Why?	1.
	2. .... Why?	2.
	3. .... Why?	3.
		4.
		5.

Meditation
- MONDAY ☐
- TUESDAY ☐
- WEDNESDAY ☐
- THURSDAY ☐
- FRIDAY ☐
- SATURDAY ☐
- SUNDAY ☐

Empty Your Brain Journal
- MONDAY ☐
- TUESDAY ☐
- WEDNESDAY ☐
- THURSDAY ☐
- FRIDAY ☐
- SATURDAY ☐
- SUNDAY ☐

WEEK 41

"Happiness is not out there to find... it's inside us."

—Sonja Lyubomirsky

FLOW CHECKER

I Am Thankful For:
1.
2.
3.
4.
5.

Acts of Kindness:
1.
2.
3.
4.
5.

PERSONAL GOAL

3 Good Things:
1.
Why?
2.
Why?
3.
Why?

Fitness Activities:
1.
2.
3.
4.
5.

Meditation
- MONDAY ☐
- TUESDAY ☐
- WEDNESDAY ☐
- THURSDAY ☐
- FRIDAY ☐
- SATURDAY ☐
- SUNDAY ☐

Empty Your Brain Journal
- MONDAY ☐
- TUESDAY ☐
- WEDNESDAY ☐
- THURSDAY ☐
- FRIDAY ☐
- SATURDAY ☐
- SUNDAY ☐

WEEK 42

"Being entirely honest with oneself is a good exercise."

—Sigmund Freud

FLOW CHECKER

PERSONAL GOAL

I Am Thankful For:
1.
2.
3.
4.
5.

3 Good Things:
1.
Why?
2.
Why?
3.
Why?

Acts of Kindness:
1.
2.
3.
4.
5.

Fitness Activities:
1.
2.
3.
4.
5.

Meditation
- MONDAY ☐
- TUESDAY ☐
- WEDNESDAY ☐
- THURSDAY ☐
- FRIDAY ☐
- SATURDAY ☐
- SUNDAY ☐

Empty Your Brain Journal
- MONDAY ☐
- TUESDAY ☐
- WEDNESDAY ☐
- THURSDAY ☐
- FRIDAY ☐
- SATURDAY ☐
- SUNDAY ☐

WEEK 43

"The happiness of your life depends upon the quality of your thoughts."

—Marcus Aurelius

FLOW CHECKER

....
....
....
....
....
....
....

I Am Thankful For:

1. ....
2. ....
3. ....
4. ....
5. ....

Acts of Kindness:

1. ....
2. ....
3. ....
4. ....
5. ....

PERSONAL GOAL

....
....
....
....
....
....
....
....
....
....
....
....
....

3 Good Things:

1. ....
Why? ....
2. ....
Why? ....
3. ....
Why? ....

Fitness Activities:

1. ....
2. ....
3. ....
4. ....
5. ....

Meditation

- MONDAY ☐
- TUESDAY ☐
- WEDNESDAY ☐
- THURSDAY ☐
- FRIDAY ☐
- SATURDAY ☐
- SUNDAY ☐

Empty Your Brain Journal

- MONDAY ☐
- TUESDAY ☐
- WEDNESDAY ☐
- THURSDAY ☐
- FRIDAY ☐
- SATURDAY ☐
- SUNDAY ☐

WEEK 44

"I am not what happened to me. I am what I choose to become."

—Carl Jung

FLOW CHECKER

I Am Thankful For:
1.
2.
3.
4.
5.

Acts of Kindness:
1.
2.
3.
4.
5.

PERSONAL GOAL

3 Good Things:
1.
Why?
2.
Why?
3.
Why?

Fitness Activities:
1.
2.
3.
4.
5.

Meditation
- MONDAY ☐
- TUESDAY ☐
- WEDNESDAY ☐
- THURSDAY ☐
- FRIDAY ☐
- SATURDAY ☐
- SUNDAY ☐

Empty Your Brain Journal
- MONDAY ☐
- TUESDAY ☐
- WEDNESDAY ☐
- THURSDAY ☐
- FRIDAY ☐
- SATURDAY ☐
- SUNDAY ☐

WEEK 45

"The universe stands aside for those people who know where they are going."

—Paulo Coelho

FLOW CHECKER

PERSONAL GOAL

I Am Thankful For:
1.
2.
3.
4.
5.

3 Good Things:
1.
Why?
2.
Why?
3.
Why?

Acts of Kindness:
1.
2.
3.
4.
5.

Fitness Activities:
1.
2.
3.
4.
5.

Meditation
- MONDAY ☐
- TUESDAY ☐
- WEDNESDAY ☐
- THURSDAY ☐
- FRIDAY ☐
- SATURDAY ☐
- SUNDAY ☐

Empty Your Brain Journal
- MONDAY ☐
- TUESDAY ☐
- WEDNESDAY ☐
- THURSDAY ☐
- FRIDAY ☐
- SATURDAY ☐
- SUNDAY ☐

WEEK 46

"A joyful life is an individual creation that cannot be copied from a recipe."

—Mihaly Csikszentmihalyi

FLOW CHECKER

I Am Thankful For:
1.
2.
3.
4.
5.

Acts of Kindness:
1.
2.
3.
4.
5.

PERSONAL GOAL

3 Good Things:
1.
Why?
2.
Why?
3.
Why?

Fitness Activities:
1.
2.
3.
4.
5.

Meditation
- MONDAY ☐
- TUESDAY ☐
- WEDNESDAY ☐
- THURSDAY ☐
- FRIDAY ☐
- SATURDAY ☐
- SUNDAY ☐

Empty Your Brain Journal
- MONDAY ☐
- TUESDAY ☐
- WEDNESDAY ☐
- THURSDAY ☐
- FRIDAY ☐
- SATURDAY ☐
- SUNDAY ☐

WEEK 47

"We need each other. The sooner we learn that it is better for us all."

—Erik Erikson

FLOW CHECKER	I Am Thankful For:	Acts of Kindness:
	1.	1.
	2.	2.
	3.	3.
	4.	4.
	5.	5.

PERSONAL GOAL	3 Good Things:	Fitness Activities:
	1. .... Why? .... 2. .... Why? .... 3. .... Why?	1. .... 2. .... 3. .... 4. .... 5. ....

Meditation
- MONDAY ☐
- TUESDAY ☐
- WEDNESDAY ☐
- THURSDAY ☐
- FRIDAY ☐
- SATURDAY ☐
- SUNDAY ☐

Empty Your Brain Journal
- MONDAY ☐
- TUESDAY ☐
- WEDNESDAY ☐
- THURSDAY ☐
- FRIDAY ☐
- SATURDAY ☐
- SUNDAY ☐

WEEK 48

"For it is in giving that we receive."

—Francis of Assisi

FLOW CHECKER

....
....
....
....
....
....

I Am Thankful For:

1. ....
2. ....
3. ....
4. ....
5. ....

Acts of Kindness:

1. ....
2. ....
3. ....
4. ....
5. ....

PERSONAL GOAL

....
....
....
....
....
....
....
....
....
....
....
....
....

3 Good Things:

1. ....
Why? ....
2. ....
Why? ....
3. ....
Why? ....

Fitness Activities:

1. ....
2. ....
3. ....
4. ....
5. ....

Meditation

- MONDAY ☐
- TUESDAY ☐
- WEDNESDAY ☐
- THURSDAY ☐
- FRIDAY ☐
- SATURDAY ☐
- SUNDAY ☐

Empty Your Brain Journal

- MONDAY ☐
- TUESDAY ☐
- WEDNESDAY ☐
- THURSDAY ☐
- FRIDAY ☐
- SATURDAY ☐
- SUNDAY ☐

WEEK 49

"There is no way to happiness. Happiness is the way."

—Thich Nhat Hanh

FLOW CHECKER

....
....
....
....
....
....
....

I Am Thankful For:

1. ....
2. ....
3. ....
4. ....
5. ....

Acts of Kindness:

1. ....
2. ....
3. ....
4. ....
5. ....

PERSONAL GOAL

....
....
....
....
....
....
....
....
....
....
....
....
....
....

3 Good Things:

1. ....
Why? ....
2. ....
Why? ....
3. ....
Why? ....

Fitness Activities:

1. ....
2. ....
3. ....
4. ....
5. ....

Meditation

- MONDAY ☐
- TUESDAY ☐
- WEDNESDAY ☐
- THURSDAY ☐
- FRIDAY ☐
- SATURDAY ☐
- SUNDAY ☐

Empty Your Brain Journal

- MONDAY ☐
- TUESDAY ☐
- WEDNESDAY ☐
- THURSDAY ☐
- FRIDAY ☐
- SATURDAY ☐
- SUNDAY ☐

WEEK 50

"Be kind whenever possible. It is always possible."

—Dalai Lama

FLOW CHECKER

I Am Thankful For:
1. ....
2. ....
3. ....
4. ....
5. ....

Acts of Kindness:
1. ....
2. ....
3. ....
4. ....
5. ....

PERSONAL GOAL

3 Good Things:
1. ....
Why? ....
2. ....
Why? ....
3. ....
Why? ....

Fitness Activities:
1. ....
2. ....
3. ....
4. ....
5. ....

Meditation
- MONDAY ☐
- TUESDAY ☐
- WEDNESDAY ☐
- THURSDAY ☐
- FRIDAY ☐
- SATURDAY ☐
- SUNDAY ☐

Empty Your Brain Journal
- MONDAY ☐
- TUESDAY ☐
- WEDNESDAY ☐
- THURSDAY ☐
- FRIDAY ☐
- SATURDAY ☐
- SUNDAY ☐

WEEK 51

"He who is brave is free."

—Lucius Annaeus Seneca

FLOW CHECKER

....
....
....
....
....
....

I Am Thankful For:

1. ....
2. ....
3. ....
4. ....
5. ....

Acts of Kindness:

1. ....
2. ....
3. ....
4. ....
5. ....

PERSONAL GOAL

....
....
....
....
....
....
....
....
....
....
....

3 Good Things:

1. ....
Why? ....
2. ....
Why? ....
3. ....
Why? ....

Fitness Activities:

1. ....
2. ....
3. ....
4. ....
5. ....

Meditation

- MONDAY ☐
- TUESDAY ☐
- WEDNESDAY ☐
- THURSDAY ☐
- FRIDAY ☐
- SATURDAY ☐
- SUNDAY ☐

Empty Your Brain Journal

- MONDAY ☐
- TUESDAY ☐
- WEDNESDAY ☐
- THURSDAY ☐
- FRIDAY ☐
- SATURDAY ☐
- SUNDAY ☐

WEEK 52

"Always believe something wonderful is about to happen."

—Unknown

FLOW CHECKER

....
....
....
....
....
....

I Am Thankful For:

1. ....
2. ....
3. ....
4. ....
5. ....

Acts of Kindness:

1. ....
2. ....
3. ....
4. ....
5. ....

PERSONAL GOAL

....
....
....
....
....
....
....
....
....
....
....
....

3 Good Things:

1. ....
Why? ....
2. ....
Why? ....
3. ....
Why? ....

Fitness Activities:

1. ....
2. ....
3. ....
4. ....
5. ....

Meditation

- MONDAY ☐
- TUESDAY ☐
- WEDNESDAY ☐
- THURSDAY ☐
- FRIDAY ☐
- SATURDAY ☐
- SUNDAY ☐

Empty Your Brain Journal

- MONDAY ☐
- TUESDAY ☐
- WEDNESDAY ☐
- THURSDAY ☐
- FRIDAY ☐
- SATURDAY ☐
- SUNDAY ☐

RECOMMENDED READING

- **Boniwell, I.** (2012). *Positive psychology in a nutshell.* McGraw-Hill Professional Publishing.
- **Cameron, J.** (2016). *The artist's way: 25th anniversary edition.* Tarcher/Penguin Putnam Inc.
- **Csikszentmihalyi, M.** (2008). *Flow: The Psychology of Optimal Experience.* Harper Perennial Modern Classics.
- **Kondo, M.** (2014). *The life-changing magic of tidying up.* Clarkson Potter/Ten Speed Press.
- **Lyubomirsky, S.** (2008). *The how of happiness.* Penguin Publishing Group.
- **Seligman, M. E. P.** (2012). *Flourish.* Atria paperback.

REFERENCES

Aman, J., Abbas, J., Nurunnabi, M., & Bano, S. (2019). The Relationship of Religiosity and Marital Satisfaction: The Role of Religious Commitment and Practices on Marital Satisfaction Among Pakistani Respondents. *Behavioral sciences (Basel, Switzerland), 9*(3), 30. https://doi.org/10.3390/bs9030030

Anderson, C. L., Monroy, M., & Keltner, D. (2018). Awe in nature heals: Evidence from military veterans, at-risk youth, and college students. *Emotion (Washington, D.C.), 18*(8), 1195-1202. https://doi.org/10.1037/emo0000442

Ano, G. G., & Vasconcelles, E. B. (2005). Religious coping and psychological adjustment to stress: A meta-analysis. *Journal of Clinical Psychology, 61*, 461-480. doi: 10.1002/jclp.20049.

Bennett, M. P., & Lengacher, C. (2009). Humor and Laughter May Influence Health IV. Humor and Immune Function. *Evidence-based complementary and alternative medicine: eCAM, 6*(2), 159-164. https://doi.org/10.1093/ecam/nem149

Bonaiuto, M., Mao, Y., Roberts, S., Psalti, A., Ariccio, S., Ganucci Cancellieri, U., & Csikszentmihalyi, M. (2016). Optimal Experience and Personal Growth: Flow and the Consolidation of Place Identity. *Frontiers in psychology, 7*, 1654. https://doi.org/10.3389/fpsyg.2016.01654

Bono, G., Emmons, R. A., & McCullough, M. E. (2004). *Gratitude in Practice and the Practice of Gratitude.* In P. A. Linley & S. Joseph (Eds.), *Positive psychology in practice* (p. 464-481). John Wiley & Sons, Inc.

Braithwaite, S. R., Selby, E. A., & Fincham, F. D. (2011). Forgiveness and relationship satisfaction: mediating mechanisms. *Journal of family psychology: JFP: journal of the Division of Family Psychology of the American Psychological Association (Division 43), 25*(4), 551-559. https://doi.org/10.1037/a0024526

Bryant, F.B. & Veroff, J. (2007). Savoring: A New Model of Positive Experience. Lawrence Erlbaum Associates, Publishers.

Cameron, J. (2017, February 7). Clearing a Path: the magic of decluttering. Retrieved from https://juliacameronlive.com/2017/02/07/clearing-a-path-the-magic-of-decluttering/

Carson, J. W., Keefe, F. J., Goli, V., Fras, A. M., Lynch, T. R., Thorp, S. R., & Buechler, J. L. (2005). Forgiveness and chronic low back pain: a preliminary study examining the relationship of forgiveness to pain, anger, and psychological distress. *The journal of pain*, 6(2), 84-91. https://doi.org/10.1016/j.jpain.2004.10.012

Chan, W. (1955) The Evolution of the Confucian Concept Jĕn. Philosophy East and West, 4(4): 295-319.

Chen, K. W., Berger, C. C., Manheimer, E., Forde, D., Magidson, J., Dachman, L., & Lejuez, C. W. (2012). Meditative therapies for reducing anxiety: a systematic review and meta-analysis of randomized controlled trials. *Depression and anxiety*, 29(7), 545-562. https://doi.org/10.1002/da.21964

Csikszentmihalyi, M. (1975). Beyond boredom and anxiety. San Francisco: Jossey-Bass Publishers.

Csikszentmihalyi, M. (1990). *Flow: The Psychology of Optimal Experience*. New York, NY: Harper and Row.

Csikszentmihalyi, M. (2004, February). *Flow, the secret to happiness* [Video]. TED Conferences. https://www.ted.com/talks/mihaly_csikszentmihalyi_flow_the_secret_to_happiness

Diener, E., Lucas, R. E., & Scollon, C. N. (2006). Beyond the hedonic treadmill: Revising the adaptation theory of well-being. *American Psychologist, 61*(4), 305-314. https://doi.org/10.1037/0003-066X.61.4.305

Doran, G. T. (1981). There's a S.M.A.R.T. Way to Write Management's Goals and Objectives. Management Review, 70, 35-36.

Eid, M., & Larsen, R. J. (Eds.). (2008). The science of subjective well-being. Guilford Press.

Emmons, R. & Mishra, A. (2011). Why Gratitude Enhances Well-Being: What We Know, and What We Need to Know. In K.M. Sheldon, T.B. Kashdan, & M.F. Steger (Eds.), *Designing Positive Psychology: Taking Stock and Moving Forward*. New York: Oxford University Press.

Emmons, R. & Stern, R. (2013). Gratitude as a Psychotherapeutic Intervention. *Journal of Clinical Psychology,* 69(8): 846-855. https://doi.org/10.1002/jclp.22020

Fincham, F. D., & Beach, S. R. (2014). I say a little prayer for you: praying for partner increases commitment in romantic relationships. *Journal of family psychology: JFP: journal of the Division of Family Psychology of the American Psychological Association (Division 43), 28*(5), 587-593. https://doi.org/10.1037/a0034999

Gable, S. & Haidt, J. (2005). What (and Why) Is Positive Psychology?. Review of General Psychology. 9. 10.1037/1089-2680.9.2.103.

Gall, T., Charbonneau, C., Clarke, N., Grant, K., Joseph, A. & Shouldice, L. (2005). Understanding the Nature and Role of Spirituality in Relation to Coping and Health: A Conceptual Framework. Canadian Psychology/Psychologie canadienne. 46. 88-104. 10.1037/h0087008.

Gaspar, J., Christie, G., Prime, D., Jolicoeur, P. & McDonald, J. (2016). Inability to suppress salient distractors predicts low visual working memory capacity. Proceedings of the National Academy of Sciences. 113. 201523471. 10.1073/pnas.1523471113.

Gaylord, S. A., Palsson, O. S., Garland, E. L., Faurot, K. R., Coble, R. S., Mann, J. D., Frey, W., Leniek, K., & Whitehead, W. E. (2011). Mindfulness training reduces the severity of irritable bowel syndrome in women: results of a randomized controlled trial. *The American journal of gastroenterology*, *106*(9), 1678-1688. https://doi.org/10.1038/ajg.2011.184

Gelkopf M. (2011). The use of humor in serious mental illness: a review. *Evidence-based complementary and alternative medicine: eCAM*, *2011*, 342837. https://doi.org/10.1093/ecam/nep106

Goldstein, C. M., Josephson, R., Xie, S., & Hughes, J. W. (2012). Current Perspectives on the Use of Meditation to Reduce Blood Pressure. *International journal of hypertension*, *2012*, 578397. https://doi.org/10.1155/2012/578397

Goyal, M., Singh, S., Sibinga, E. M., Gould, N. F., Rowland-Seymour, A., Sharma, R., Berger, Z., Sleicher, D., Maron, D. D., Shihab, H. M., Ranasinghe, P. D., Linn, S., Saha, S., Bass, E. B., & Haythornthwaite, J. A. (2014). Meditation Programs for Psychological Stress and Well-being: A Systematic Review and Meta-analysis. *JAMA internal medicine*, *174*(3), 357-368. https://doi.org/10.1001/jamainternmed.2013.13018

Greater Good Science Center (2018, September). *The Science of Awe* [White Paper]. https://ggsc.berkeley.edu/images/uploads/GGSC-JTF_White_Paper-Awe_FINAL.pdf?_ga=2.134453810.2139496609.1623998312-243405621.1623209178

Griskevicius, V., Shiota, M. N., & Neufeld, S. L. (2010). Influence of different positive emotions on persuasion processing: A functional evolutionary approach. *Emotion (Washington, D.C.)*, *10*(2), 190-206. https://doi.org/10.1037/a0018421

Grossman, P., Niemann, L., Schmidt, S., & Walach, H. (2004). Mindfulness-based stress reduction and health benefits: A meta-analysis. In: Database of Abstracts of Reviews of Effects (DARE): Quality-assessed Reviews [Internet]. York, United Kingdom: Centre for Reviews and Dissemination.

Hall, E. (2019, January 31). Aristotle's Pursuit of Happiness. *Wall Street Journal*. https://www.wsj.com/articles/aristotles-pursuit-of-happiness-11548950094

Harvard Health Publishing (2011). Giving thanks can make you happier. Accessed on June 1, 2021 from https://www.health.harvard.edu/healthbeat/giving-thanks-can-make-you-happier

Helliwell, John F., Richard Layard, Jeffrey Sachs, and Jan-Emmanuel De Neve, eds. 2020. World Happiness Report 2020. New York: Sustainable Development Solutions Network.

Hurley, D. & Kwon, P. (2012). Results of a Study to Increase Savoring the Moment: Differential Impact on Positive and Negative Outcomes. Journal of Happiness Studies, 13. 10.1007/s10902-011-9280-8.

Jedel, S., Hoffman, A., Merriman, P., Swanson, B., Voigt, R., Rajan, K. B., Shaikh, M., Li, H., & Keshavarzian, A. (2014). A randomized controlled trial of mindfulness-based stress reduction to prevent flare-up in patients with inactive ulcerative colitis. *Digestion*, 89(2), 142-155. https://doi.org/10.1159/000356316

Jose, P., Lim, B. & Bryant, F. (2012). Does savoring increase happiness? A daily diary study. The Journal of Positive Psychology. 7. 176-187. 10.1080/17439760.2012.671345.

Keltner, D. (Host). (2021, February 21). Are You Setting the Right Goals? (No. 84) [Audio Podcast Episode]. In *The Science of Happiness*. Greater Good Science Center. https://greatergood.berkeley.edu/podcasts/item/are_you_setting_the_right_goals

Keng, S. L., Smoski, M. J., & Robins, C. J. (2011). Effects of mindfulness on psychological health: a review of empirical studies. *Clinical psychology review*, 31(6), 1041-1056. https://doi.org/10.1016/j.cpr.2011.04.006

Kennelly, S. (2012 July). 10 Steps to Savoring the Good Things in Life. Greater Good Magazine. Retrieved from https://greatergood.berkeley.edu/article/item/10_steps_to_savoring_the_good_things_in_life

Koenig H. G. (2012). Religion, spirituality, and health: the research and clinical implications. *ISRN psychiatry*, 2012, 278730. https://doi.org/10.5402/2012/278730

Kondo, M. & Hirano, C. (2014). *The Life-Changing Magic of Tidying Up: The Japanese art of decluttering and organizing.* Ten Speed Press.

Kurtz, L. E., & Algoe, S. B. (2017). When sharing a laugh means sharing more: Testing the role of shared laughter on short-term interpersonal consequences. *Journal of Nonverbal Behavior, 41*(1), 45-65. https://doi.org/10.1007/s10919-016-0245-9

Kusner, K. G., Mahoney, A., Pargament, K. I., & DeMaris, A. (2014). Sanctification of marriage and spiritual intimacy predicting observed marital interactions across the transition to parenthood. *Journal of Family Psychology, 28*(5), 604-614. https://doi.org/10.1037/a0036989

Lee, M. A., & Kawachi, I. (2019). The keys to happiness: Associations between personal values regarding core life domains and happiness in South Korea. *PloS one, 14*(1), e0209821. https://doi.org/10.1371/journal.pone.0209821

Lench, H. C., Levine, L. J., Dang, V., Kaiser, K. A., Carpenter, Z. K., Carlson, S. J., Flynn, E., Perez, K. A., & Winckler, B. (2021). Optimistic expectations have benefits for effort and emotion with little cost. *Emotion.* Advance online publication. https://doi.org/10.1037/emo0000957

Louie, D., Brook, K., & Frates, E. (2016). The Laughter Prescription: A Tool for Lifestyle Medicine. *American journal of lifestyle medicine, 10*(4), 262-267. https://doi.org/10.1177/1559827614550279

Luo, S.(2019) Happiness and the Good Life: A Classical Confucian Perspective. *Dao* 18: 41-58. https://doi.org/10.1007/s11712-018-9640-8

Lyubomirsky, S., Sheldon, K. M., & Schkade, D. (2005). Pursuing happiness: The architecture of sustainable change. *Review of General Psychology, 9*(2), 111-131. https://doi.org/10.1037/1089-2680.9.2.111

Lyubomirsky, S. (2007). *The How of Happiness: A Scientific Approach to Getting the Life You Want.* Piatkus Books.

Mao Y., Roberts S., Pagliaro S., Csikszentmihalyi M., Bonaiuto M. (2016). Optimal Experience and optimal identity: a multinational study of the associations between flow and social identity. *Personal. Soc. Psychol.* 7:67. 10.3389/fpsyg.2016.00067

Marks, M. J., Trafimow, D., Busche, L. K., & Oates, K. N. (2013). A Function of Forgiveness: Exploring the Relationship Between Negative Mood and Forgiving. SAGE Open. https://doi.org/10.1177/2158244013507267

Marsh, J. (2012, March 14). Kristin Neff on The Power of Self-Compassion. Greater Good Magazine. https://greatergood.berkeley.edu/article/item/the_power_of_self_compassion

McCosker, B., & Moran, C. C. (2012). Differential effects of self-esteem and interpersonal competence on humor styles. *Psychology research and behavior management, 5,* 143-150. https://doi.org/10.2147/PRBM.S36967

McGonigal, K. (2019). *The Joy of Movement: How exercise helps us find happiness, hope, connection, and courage.* Penguin Press.

McMahon, D. M. (2006). *Happiness: A history.* Atlantic Monthly Press.

Mesmer-Magnus, J. & Glew, D. & Viswesvaran, C. (2012). A meta-analysis of positive humor in the workplace. Journal of Managerial Psychology. 27. 155-190. 10.1108/02683941211199554

Neff, K. (2011, May 27). Why Self-Compassion Trumps Self-Esteem. Greater Good Magazine. https://greatergood.berkeley.edu/article/item/try_selfcompassion/

Neff, K. (2011). Self-Compassion: The proven power of being kind to yourself. William Borrow.

News in Health (2019). Practicing Gratitude: Ways to Improve Positivity. Accessed on June 1, 2021 from.https://newsinhealth.nih.gov/2019/03/practicing-gratitude

No Author (2009). The History of Utilitarianism. Stanford Encyclopedia of Philosophy. Retrieved on June 8, 2021 from https://plato.stanford.edu/entries/utilitarianism-history/

No author (n.d.). The 24 Character Strengths. VIA Institute on Character. Retrieved from https://www.viacharacter.org/character-strengths

Park, N., Peterson, C., (2016). Positive Psychology and Physical Health: Research and Applications. American Journal of Lifestyle Medicine. 10(3): 200-206.

Parks, A. C., Della Porta, M. D., Pierce, R. S., Zilca, R., & Lyubomirsky, S. (2012). Pursuing Happiness in Everyday Life: The Characteristics and Behaviors of Online Happiness Seekers. Emotion. Advance online publication. Doi: 10.1037/a0028587

Pérez-Aranda, A., Hofmann, J., Feliu-Soler, A., Ramírez-Maestre, C., Andrés-Rodríguez, L., Ruch, W., & Luciano, J. V. (2019). Laughing away the pain: A narrative review of humour, sense of humour and pain. *European journal of pain (London, England), 23*(2), 220-233. https://doi.org/10.1002/ejp.1309

Peterson, C. (2009). Positive Psychology. Reclaiming Children and Youth. 18(2): 3-7.

Peterson, Christopher & Seligman, M.E.P. (2004). Character Strengths and Virtues: A Handbook and Classification. Washington, D.C.: APA Press and Oxford University Press.

Phelps, C. L., Paniagua, S. M., Willcockson, I. U., & Potter, J. S. (2018). The relationship between self-compassion and the risk for substance use disorder. *Drug and alcohol dependence*, *183*, 78-81. https://doi.org/10.1016/j.drugalcdep.2017.10.026

Piff, P. K., Dietze, P., Feinberg, M., Stancato, D. M., & Keltner, D. (2015). Awe, the small self, and prosocial behavior. Journal of Personality and Social Psychology, 108(6), 883-899.

Rasic, D. T., Belik, S. L., Elias, B., Katz, L. Y., Enns, M., Sareen, J., & Swampy Cree Suicide Prevention Team (2009). Spirituality, religion and suicidal behavior in a nationally representative sample. *Journal of affective disorders*, *114*(1-3), 32-40. https://doi.org/10.1016/j.jad.2008.08.007

Reiner, K., Tibi, L., & Lipsitz, J. D. (2013). Do mindfulness-based interventions reduce pain intensity? A critical review of the literature. *Pain medicine (Malden, Mass.)*, *14*(2), 230-242. https://doi.org/10.1111/pme.12006

Robertson, C. L., Ishibashi, K., Chudzynski, J., Mooney, L. J., Rawson, R. A., Dolezal, B. A., Cooper, C. B., Brown, A. K., Mandelkern, M. A., & London, E. D. (2016). Effect of Exercise Training on Striatal Dopamine D2/D3 Receptors in Methamphetamine Users during Behavioral Treatment. *Neuropsychopharmacology: official publication of the American College of Neuropsychopharmacology*, *41*(6), 1629-1636. https://doi.org/10.1038/npp.2015.331

Rohrer, J. M., Richter, D., Brümmer, M., Wagner, G. G., & Schmukle, S. C. (2018). Successfully Striving for Happiness: Socially Engaged Pursuits Predict Increases in Life Satisfaction. Psychological science, 29(8), 1291-1298. https://doi.org/10.1177/0956797618761660

Rook, K. S., & Charles, S. T. (2017). Close social ties and health in later life: Strengths and vulnerabilities. *The American psychologist*, *72*(6), 567-577. https://doi.org/10.1037/amp0000104

Roster, C., Ferrari, J. & Jurkat, M. (2016). The dark side of home: Assessing possession 'clutter' on subjective well-being. Journal of Environmental Psychology. 46. 10.1016/j.jenvp.2016.03.003.

Rudd, M., Vohs, K. D., & Aaker, J. (2012). Awe expands people's perception of time, alters decision making, and enhances well-being. Psychological science, 23(10), 1130-1136. https://doi.org/10.1177/0956797612438731

Sansone, R. A., & Sansone, L. A. (2010). Gratitude and well being: the benefits of appreciation. *Psychiatry*, 7(11): 18-22.

Saxbe, D. E., & Repetti, R. (2010). No Place Like Home: Home Tours Correlate With Daily Patterns of Mood and Cortisol. Personality and Social Psychology Bulletin, 36(1), 71-81. https://doi.org/10.1177/0146167209352864

Sbarra, D. A., Smith, H. L., & Mehl, M. R. (2012). When leaving your ex, love yourself: observational ratings of self-compassion predict the course of emotional recovery following marital separation. *Psychological science, 23*(3), 261-269. https://doi.org/10.1177/0956797611429466

Seligman, M., Parks, A. & Steen, T. (2004). A balanced psychology and a full life. Philosophical Transactions of the Royal Society. 359: 1379-1381.

Seligman, M., Steen, T., Park, N. & Peterson, C. (2005). Positive Psychology Progress: Empirical Validation of Interventions. American Psychologist. 60(5): 410-421.

Seligman, M. E. P. (2002). Authentic happiness: Using the new positive psychology to realize your potential for lasting fulfillment. New York: Free Press.

Sheldon, K., Boehm, J., & Lyubomirsky, S. (2013). Variety is the Spice of Happiness: The Hedonic Adaptation Prevention Model. In I. Boniwell, S. David, & A.C. Ayers (Eds.). *Oxford Handbook of Happiness. Oxford University Press.*

Sheldon, K.M. & Lyubomirsky, S. (2006) How to increase and sustain positive emotion: The effects of expressing gratitude and visualizing best possible selves. *The Journal of Positive Psychology*, 1(20: 73-82, DOI: 10.1080/17439760500510676

Stellar, J. E., Gordon, A., Anderson, C. L., Piff, P. K., McNeil, G. D., & Keltner, D. (2018). Awe and humility. *Journal of personality and social psychology, 114*(2), 258-269. https://doi.org/10.1037/pspi0000109

Stellar, J. E., John-Henderson, N., Anderson, C. L., Gordon, A. M., McNeil, G. D., & Keltner, D. (2015). Positive affect and markers of inflammation: Discrete positive emotions predict lower levels of inflammatory cytokines. *Emotion, 15*(2), 129-133. https://doi.org/10.1037/emo0000033

Toussaint, L., Shields, G. S., Dorn, G., & Slavich, G. M. (2016). Effects of lifetime stress exposure on mental and physical health in young adulthood: How stress degrades and forgiveness protects health. *Journal of health psychology, 21*(6), 1004-1014. https://doi.org/10.1177/1359105314544132

University of California Berkeley Greater Good in Action. (n.d.). Random Acts of Kindness. Retrieved June 1, 2021, from file:///home/chronos/u-9ad5a3bcd9a3b0dd639d8dcceae836559e3d4914/MyFiles/Downloads/practice_random_acts_of_kindness.pdf

Vaillant, G. E. (2012). *Triumphs of experience: The men of the Harvard Grant Study.* The Belknap Press of Harvard University Press. https://doi.org/10.4159/harvard.9780674067424

Vartanian, L. R., Kernan, K. M., & Wansink, B. (2017). Clutter, Chaos, and Overconsumption: The Role of Mind-Set in Stressful and Chaotic Food Environments. Environment and Behavior, 49(2), 215-223. https://doi.org/10.1177/0013916516628178

Waldinger, R. (2015, January). *What makes a good life? Lessons from the longest study on happiness* [Video]. TED Conferences. https://www.ted.com/talks/robert_waldinger_what_makes_a_good_life_lessons_from_the_longest_study_on_happiness

Wellenzohn, S., Proyer, R. T., & Ruch, W. (2018). Who Benefits From Humor-Based Positive Psychology Interventions? The Moderating Effects of Personality Traits and Sense of Humor. *Frontiers in psychology*, 9, 821. https://doi.org/10.3389/fpsyg.2018.00821

Wilson, J.T. (2006). Brightening the Mind: The Impact of Practicing Gratitude on Focus and Resilience in Learning. *Journal of the Scholarship of Teaching and Learning, 16(4): 1-13. doi: 10.14434/josotl.v16i4.19998*

Windle, G., Hughes, D., Linck, P., Russell, I. & Woods, B. (2010) Is exercise effective in promoting mental well-being in older age? A systematic review, Aging & Mental Health, 14:6, 652-669, DOI: 10.1080/13607861003713232

Xiv, D. L., & Cutler, H. C. (1999). The Art of Happiness. Hodder Paperback.

Yim J. (2016). Therapeutic Benefits of Laughter in Mental Health: A Theoretical Review. *The Tohoku journal of experimental medicine*, 239(3), 243-249. https://doi.org/10.1620/tjem.239.243

Zacher, H., & Rudolph, C. W. (2021). Individual differences and changes in subjective wellbeing during the early stages of the COVID-19 pandemic. *American Psychologist, 76*(1), 50-62. http://dx.doi.org/10.1037/amp0000702

Ziv, A. (1976). Facilitating effects of humor on creativity. *Journal of Educational Psychology, 68*(3), 318-322. https://doi.org/10.1037/0022-0663.68.3.318

Made in the USA
Las Vegas, NV
02 August 2024